To Joe,

A Great Giants Fan!

63

LIFE ON THE LINE

LIFE ON THE LINE

By KARL NELSON
& BARRY STANTON

WRS
PUBLISHING

A Division of WRS Group, Inc.
Waco, Texas

First published in the United States of America in 1993 by WRS Publishing, A Division of WRS Group, Inc., 701 N. New Road, Waco, Texas 76710
Book design by Kenneth Turbeville
Jacket design by Talmage Minter

10 9 8 7 6 5 4 3 2

Library of Congress Catalog Card Number

Nelson, Karl, 1960–
      Life on the line / by Karl Nelson & Barry Stanton.
            p.   cm.
      ISBN 1-56796-051-0 : $19.95
      1. Nelson, Karl, 1960–   . 2. Football players—United States—
Biography. 3. Cancer—Patients—United States—Biography.
I. Stanton, Barry, 1955–   . II. Title.
GV939.N38A3 1993
796.332'092—dc20
      [B]   93-27769
                                                                                CIP

Heidi—
You are the light that got me to
the end of the tunnel
that is still shining bright,

and

To all the people who had
cancer before me,
those who survived and
those who did not—
for testing the treatments which
allowed me to be a survivor.

—Karl Nelson

Dedication

To Barbara and Michael. Everything I do, I do for you.

—BJS

Acknowledgments

This author would like to thank Jay Goldberg, our agent, for the absolutely tireless effort that would not let this project disappear; Harvey Araton, Hank Gola and Bill Pennington for their advice; Marilynn and Seymour Stanton, for "Grandma and Grandpa's Finest Baby-sitting Service"; Dr. Jerome Horowitz for the use of his laser printer; and, finally, Marilyn Horowitz for an inspiration that stayed with me. I hope I've made you all proud.

—BJS

Acknowledgments

Cancer is something that most people who have been through want to forget. They want to block it out of their memory. If it weren't for Heidi's recollection, I think this book would be only fifty pages long. Bringing back the memories, the nights we lay in bed asking questions we couldn't answer, created some additional nights with some of the same questions and thoughts. It was a painful process, and I'm very fortunate to have had Heidi with me, going through it yet again.

Ever since I beat Hodgkin's the first time, people have told me what a great book my story would make. I finally wrote that book, but I could not have done it without my true friend and agent, Jay Goldberg. Even though "everyone" thought it was a great idea, Jay worked two long years before our dream became a reality. I believe this book can help people, but without Jay's efforts, it would not have been published.

We are appreciative of our friends and family, and especially of my daughters, Brittany and Lyndsay, for giving us the support when we needed it, and space when we didn't. God has blessed me with many gifts. Among those gifts I include my family and friends.

In the "How To" chapter of this book, I describe what to look for in a doctor. Dr. David Wolf embodies all the qualities I think are essential to get one through the ordeal of cancer and on with the rest of their life. He is doctor, confidant, and friend.

A special thank you to Dr. Wayman Spence of WRS Publishing for having the vision to see something in my story that no other publisher did. He understood that this book was worth publishing and it can be an inspiration to many people. My true gratitude to his wonderful staff including Sherry Claypool, Terri Johnson, Ann Page, and Georgia Brady.

Football is a tough game played by tough men. It takes a tough person to coach this game. There are parts of this book in which Bill Parcells may not come across in a positive light. He treated me in certain ways at certain times because he thought he was doing the right thing for me. I didn't always agree with him, but I certainly respect him. He was my only professional coach, and I couldn't have asked for a better one. He teaches a lot more than football, if you are willing to listen.

If I had not been drafted by the New York Giants, this book would not have such a happy ending. They stood by me every step of the way. Thank you.

—Karl Nelson

Table of Contents

Foreword
By Bill Parcells

I always put a tremendous amount of pressure on my offensive tackles. Karl knows that. He's very perceptive.

The tackles are the guys who are going to expose the quarterback. And when Karl was playing for me, most of the more damaging players on our opponents' defenses were going against him. They were the guys who could ruin a game for the Giants. So I put a lot of pressure on him.

Nelson and Brad Benson, our other tackle, were always aware that I knew what they were facing. I'd remind them in practice; we'd talk about it. Who it was, what they had to do. That's what the game is. It's a team game, but there are individual battles. Sometimes, the eight or nine other guys can't win theirs unless you win yours.

When we drafted Karl in 1983, he really wasn't ready to compete on a professional level. He was behind when it came to strength and stamina, things like that.

I thought he had ability, but you never really know. A player who's not in good shape coming in usually has problems somewhere down the line. On the other hand, he was smart. And when we started our off-season training program, he jumped right in.

By '84, he was starting to show promise. He was tall, with long arms and good balance, and he was always a pretty good run blocker. We made the playoffs that season and by then he was really coming along. He was on his way.

In '85, he was a pretty good tackle. He had a few problems in the individual battles but he was going against top-line guys in the NFC East: Charles Mann of the Washington Redskins, Reggie White of the Philadelphia Eagles and Ed "Too Tall" Jones of the Dallas Cowboys. And it wasn't too long before he was holding his own.

In '86, he only had one bad game, against Jacob Green of the Seattle Seahawks. That was the last game we lost that year. I still remember it. He was wearing his emotions on his sleeve, and I really hammered at that with him.

"Guys like Lawrence Taylor feed off that," I told him. "They see you frustrated and that just gets them going."

A lot of our running game went to the right side that year, running Joe Morris behind Karl and Mark Bavaro, our tight end. Billy Ard was our left guard and we used him to pull around, so we had Karl and Bavaro and Ard and Maurice Carthon, our fullback, at the point of attack. That won us a Super Bowl.

Then of course we had the problem. I knew Karl's shoulder was bothering him. Then, all of a sudden, the doctors found that other thing.

As a coach, you can only do so much, add so much. And in Karl's case it was very exasperating.

Now that I've gone through an open-heart surgery, I think you have to face these things alone. You have the support from the people who love you, but those people don't have the problem. You do. You're the one who has to go through it. I could only support Karl from the standpoint of the organization, and try to provide whatever he needed. I think we did that.

His comeback in '88 was probably more difficult for me than it was for him. If I'd been very different than I always was, he would have noticed. He would have felt I was feeling sorry for him. And I knew he'd be able to tell. He knew me. We'd been standing in that huddle in practice with each other for five years.

The last thing he needed from me was sympathy. So I used to tell him, "Well, we're going to hang a purple flag on the tower today. That's the sympathy banner. Karl Nelson's practicing today."

I tried very hard not to be different. Sometimes I noticed the other players saying, "Geez, you've got to give this guy a break."

But I couldn't.

I knew it was a battle for him. He wasn't quite the same guy. He knew and I knew. I tried to be as positive as I could when I saw progress, when I saw that things were getting better. But I wasn't trying to fool him. I wasn't playing a game.

When he was going through the chemotherapy, I'd see him in the shower with that rope hanging from his chest, the tube or the catheter or whatever it's called. And he'd wear that wig. But I'd never not look him in the eye.

Karl is a very brave guy. I admire him. I never told him that, but I did. We never really talked about it. He came back to a point, then he got hurt in the second game of '88. And I found myself asking, "When is this kid going to get a break?"

These kids—well, they were really men—were a special group. Nelson, Brad Benson, Chris Godfrey, Billy Ard, Bart Oates, they were very similar people. They were tough and smart and prideful.

Being in that locker room is a special thing. It brought me back into coaching with the New England Patriots. It can get you, and it got me, with the nerves and the smoking. But what you have there is very special and you can't get it anywhere else, especially when they call you champions.

I had great admiration for Karl. He's an interesting guy. And he could have been—if he hadn't been robbed of it—one of the top guys in the league. Certainly he was, at the end of '86, and I think he would have improved more.

Players are always talking about this guy being a great player, or that guy being a great player. "Great" is overused. I'd rather be reserved and not say "great." I'd rather say he was better than good.

But he had his place in the sun and he, along with the others, accomplished some things that only a few have done.

Hey, I loved the kid. I think he knew that.

And he escaped.

Chapter 1
Cancer, Again

I walked into the house, put a bucket of Roy Rogers' fried chicken on the table, turned to my wife and said, "It's back."

Heidi didn't have time to cry. At 7:30 p.m., people would start arriving for our annual Christmas party and it was already 7:20.

We really wanted to have that party. The past year had taught us to appreciate what we have, and we wanted to share that with our friends.

We were, in a way, celebrating my "victory" over Hodgkin's disease.

The cancer had been discovered in the summer of 1987, just seven months after I reached the top of my game as the starting right tackle for the New York Giants in our win over the Denver Broncos in Super Bowl XXI. I went for arthroscopic surgery on my injured left shoulder in August and that's when, in a routine X-ray, they found it.

Cancer.

But I fought the Hodgkin's, a cancer that attacks the lymphatic system, with radiation treatments, and made it back to play for the Giants again in 1988. The comeback ended with a last-minute loss to the Jets that knocked us out of a playoff spot. Still, the Nelsons had plenty to be thankful for, so we planned our party for December 20, two days after the season ended.

That's the day we realized the cancer was back.

It had been a week since my doctor had found a lump in my neck during a checkup.

It was a scheduled checkup, but something I would have put off until after the season was over if I hadn't been feeling a little tired in late December. Football players, notorious for

ignoring and overcoming pain, are not the best at judging
their own medical condition. I was taking medication for my
thyroid, which had been destroyed during the radiation
treatments I'd had the year before. I assumed that the
medication needed to be adjusted, that the dosage needed to
be increased. That had done the trick before. Or maybe it was
just that lingering cold I'd been unable to shake.

But cancer? Again?

The thought hadn't crossed my conscious mind.

We'd had that one more game to play and I tried to
concentrate on that. Then we lost that last game to the Jets,
27–21, and held our season-ending team meeting on Tuesday,
the same day we'd scheduled our party. When the meeting
ended, I drove directly from Giants Stadium in New Jersey
through the Lincoln Tunnel to Manhattan and Dr. David Wolf's
office on 61st Street.

Once I got there, I waited. Dr. Wolf, like most doctors who
treat cancer, is, unfortunately, extremely busy. It's not as if
you make a 1 p.m. appointment and you walk into his office
at 1:05. It doesn't work that way.

I sat in his "waiting room," four chairs in front of the
elevator on Wolf's floor. I don't remember sitting there thinking
the worst. Heidi says I'm just not like that, and she's right. I'm
an optimist, not a pessimist.

I still thought it was an infection or a swollen gland, and I
thought this was a follow-up visit to give me the results of my
blood tests. I wasn't expecting anything bad when I walked
into Dr. Wolf's office. The doctor poked and prodded at the
lump in my neck. Then he delivered the shocker.

"We've reviewed all of your blood tests," he told me. "I've
ruled out an infection. I want to take out the lump and find
out what it is."

That's when it hit me. I knew what it was.

"Is it back?" I asked him.

He said, "It may be or it may be something else. That's why
I want to take it out."

I asked him what the odds were, and he said, "50–50."

But I could tell by the way he said it that the odds weren't
nearly that much in my favor. I knew by the tone of his voice
and by the way he was acting.

Then I had to tell Heidi.

In 1987, the first time I found out I had cancer, Giants
physician Dr. Russ Warren broke the news to Heidi. He tried to

explain things as much as possible, but she was shocked and confused. She got ready as fast as she could, jumped in the car and raced through the streets to pick up a friend who was going with her to the hospital in New York.

She made a wrong turn, though, and ended up on a street in a nearby town where we had owned our first house together. She had no idea how she'd gotten there. She stopped and looked at our old house, wondering, how things could change so quickly.

This time, I knew I couldn't tell her over the phone. I still had a CAT scan scheduled at New York Hospital. It was already five o'clock, so I called just to say I'd be too late to help with the last-minute party preparations. She gave me the order for the bucket of chicken and I dutifully stopped at Roy Rogers to pick up a meal I knew we wouldn't eat.

I have a 50–50 chance that it's nothing, I told myself on the ride home. But, with the way I'm feeling, I'm not optimistic. If it's not cancer, why does he want to take it out? And why does he want to take it out as soon as possible?

The optimist wasn't optimistic. That was a telling sign.

Paper plates were set on the table when I got home. Heidi was sitting in her chair, the same chair she always sat in, the same one she still sits in, when I gave her the news.

"Dr. Wolf wants to take the lump out," I said.

"When?" Heidi asked.

"As soon as possible."

The doorbell rang. Dave and Marge D'Anna, our first guests, had arrived.

"When I opened the door, I just had to try to keep from breaking out in tears," Heidi said. "It was kind of hard, especially since Margie's sister was dying of cancer."

The party started. I really don't remember much about the whole night. I kept my poker face and could have gone the whole night and not told anybody. I don't let outside things affect me. Football has taught me to control my emotions. Former Giants coach Bill Parcells has stressed that. If an opponent beats you—and, sooner or later, one will—don't show it, don't let him know it.

Heidi, eight-months pregnant with our second child, had to let it out. She told some people, didn't tell others.

"Certain people I had to let know," she said. "Others, I couldn't. I would smile to one person and cry to the next. It went on all night. Sad. And very strange."

She chose to tell the friends that she knew she couldn't keep it from, and kept it from the rest. She spent the night running upstairs to the bathroom every twenty minutes, allegedly to fix her makeup, but really just to be alone.

Until, finally, we were.

It was just after midnight. The guests had all left, the ones who knew staying just a little longer than the ones who didn't. Heidi and I had cleaned up our home and were alone, together, in bed.

"Karl, what do you think? Seriously."

"Heidi, I think it's back. I really do."

I thought back. I was tired, and it wasn't just the thyroid medication. I'd been waking up in the middle of the night, sweating. Now I recognized those symptoms.

I hadn't let myself put the puzzle together, but now I knew it was cancer, and so did Heidi.

"When these doctors say 'It could be,' then it already is," Heidi told me. "And you know that."

The next day, I got up and headed to Giants Stadium to film a commercial for Abraham & Straus, the New York department store. That's where I got a call from Heidi, telling me that I had an appointment with Dr. John Whitsel II, a surgeon and one of Wolf's associates at New York Hospital, who would remove the lump.

I finished the shoot and headed back again, through the Lincoln Tunnel. Meanwhile, Heidi played media host.

Norman Ross, a producer for WYNY-TV in New York, was working on a piece called "Unsung Heroes of Sports," about athletes who work for charities. We had been active with the Tomorrows Children's Fund, a group that works with young cancer patients, even before my first bout with the disease, so I guess we were a natural selection.

Ross and his camera crew showed up in the late afternoon, expecting to find Heidi and me. Instead, they got Heidi and Brittany, our then-two-year-old daughter. Heidi stalled them until I got home from Dr. Whitsel's office.

On camera, Heidi was uncharacteristically cool. In the segment focusing on our special Christmas, she gave no indication of our latest trials. It came off as a story of two people who have battled cancer together and are happy for what they've got.

There's no clue about what we were going through. Nothing, except her last words:

"You just have to hope for the best," she told the camera, "and hope there's a little guardian angel watching on your shoulder."

Heidi was counting on it, even if she had her doubts. Our second daughter, Lyndsay, was due January 12, but Heidi remembers, "I just felt that God gives and God takes. Here I was having this baby and Karl had cancer again. For the first time in my life, I'd gotten exactly what I'd wanted, and Karl was it. I didn't ask for the second baby. We thought Karl was sterile after the radiation treatments. I was perfectly happy with Karl and Brittany. I felt like I was going to have another baby and lose him. I feel terrible when I say that now, because I love Lyndsay so much. When they handed her to me, I was thrilled to have a baby in my arms. But I knew what I really wanted in my arms. It was Karl."

And she felt she was in definite danger of losing me again, although I never felt that way.

This sounds backwards, but before I got sick the first time, I had always been afraid of dying. Then I got sick, and I wasn't afraid anymore. It's not as if I'm looking forward to it. But I used to get anxiety attacks thinking about death, and I don't anymore. I know you just can't tell what lies ahead.

In December of 1988, just before Christmas, I knew that radiation therapy hadn't beaten my Hodgkin's, not completely. And I knew chemotherapy was the next step.

Some cancer patients say it's worse the second time around. The first time, they'll tell you, you accept the disease and just want to know what you have to do to beat it.

The second time the cancer comes back, you feel you've already fought the good fight. You've done what you've been told, and you've found out it wasn't enough.

That's when some people give up. But I didn't. That's not the way I'm made. For as long as I'd been a football player, I'd done what my coaches told me to do to overcome the obstacles in front of me. Cancer, even a second time, was just another obstacle to overcome.

I was more apprehensive, though. The first time, I had football to get me through. Everything was "When can I play again?" The second time, I said to hell with football. I just wanted to get this taken care of, do whatever I had to do to be a husband to Heidi and a father for my kids.

It was a little easier, because I knew it was treatable and I knew a little bit about what I was getting into. But it was harder, too, because now I really knew what I was getting into. I knew what the treatments would be and that chemo was harder than radiation. But I was doing a typical "hope for the best," which I'm famous for. You just can't start asking yourself, Why me? I kept my normal attitude, which was, What do I have to do to get better?

I was still being the good football soldier, ready to take orders from my coaches.

After all, I'd already seen that pay off, on and off the field.

Chapter 2
Super Bowl XXI

I didn't enjoy Super Bowl XXI. I really didn't. That's the biggest regret of my football career, that I didn't enjoy the Super Bowl. Not one bit.

My first thought after the game was to get to the locker room and get changed as fast as I could. I knew the locker rooms at the Rose Bowl were so small it would be a zoo with all the media in there and I didn't want to put up with that.

So while Brad Benson and Chris Godfrey, my linemates, carried Parcells off the field, I just shook hands with Rulon Jones, the Broncos' defensive end, and quickly left.

That season, our team was focused on winning. Once we made the playoffs, we had to win the division. Once we won the division, we had to finish with the best record in the NFC to get the home-field advantage during the playoffs.

Once we got that, we had to keep winning. We got to the conference championship game, then we had to make the Super Bowl. And once we made it to the Super Bowl, just getting there wasn't enough. We had to win.

The team stayed very focused, and I, especially, did. I stayed focused on the next step.

Then, all of a sudden, the Super Bowl was over. And all I could think of was, well, who do we play now?

It's hard to explain, but getting to the top of the mountain is much more satisfying than being on the top of the mountain. Once we were there, I just couldn't believe it. It was like, is that all there is? This can't be it.

The whole Super Bowl experience is kind of a blank for me. I remember we were staying at a pretty nice hotel, the Westin South Coast Plaza in Costa Mesa, California. There were a lot of people around. A lot of Giants fans in the lobby. It got so crowded that it would take an hour just to get from the front door to the elevator if you stopped and signed every autograph. I'd pick up Brittany and rush through the lobby, using her like a shield so the fans would let me alone. My free time was limited and I wanted to spend as much of it as I could with my family.

During the week, there were media sessions. There was an optional one on Monday night, when we got to our hotel, but I didn't go because I didn't have to. We'd just flown in and I didn't feel like it.

Tuesday we had to suit up in our game jerseys and pants and hold Picture Day at Orange Coast College in Costa Mesa. That was a waste of time unless you were Phil Simms, our quarterback, or Lawrence Taylor, our linebacker and the league's Most Valuable Player. Nobody wanted to take pictures of a right tackle.

Then there were one-hour media sessions back at the hotel on Wednesday and Thursday mornings. The NFL puts every player at a table, with a name card so people know who you are. I'd just sit at my table talking to the other offensive lineman. Nobody wanted to talk to us, so we'd interview each other.

When somebody did come by, it was always to ask about Simms or Joe Morris or one of our stars. And that was fine with me. Hey, I'm an offensive lineman. We don't need recognition, and we usually don't get it. Besides, I didn't want to get too excited. When I get too excited I don't play well. Too much nervous tension.

Heidi was interviewed that week more than I was. She grew up in New Jersey and a lot of people thought that made a good angle for their human-interest stories.

We had a good week there. Practice was very intense. We did a lot more hitting than I thought we would and were going at a higher tempo. Things got so crazy I almost got into a fight with Jim Burt, our nose tackle.

Then, the Saturday night before the game, they moved us to the Beverly Garland Hotel in Hollywood. We had seen that on our itinerary and thought, Wow! This will be a really great hotel!

It turned out that the Beverly Garland was a Howard Johnson's. We spent the night before the game at a Howard Johnson's and I had my Saturday night meal at the Howard Johnson's and my Sunday pre-game meal at the Howard Johnson's. It was not exactly what I had expected before the Super Bowl.

We tried to follow the same routine as much as possible and Bill wanted to get us away from all the fans who had been waiting since 1963 for their team to get back to the NFL's championship game.

I roomed with Brad Benson, our left tackle. When we had beaten the Washington Redskins down at RFK Stadium, Brad had had a one-on-one duel with Dexter Manley, the Redskins' star defensive end. And Brad had this big cut on his nose where it kept getting smashed by his face mask. John Madden, the CBS commentator, took one look at that nose with a big band-aid on it and blood trickling down, and he went wild. That band-aid got Brad the NFL's "Offensive Player of the Week" and it got him into the Pro Bowl.

As a roommate, though, Brad was a pain in the ass. He didn't want to go to bed before games. He wanted to stay up and talk. Then he had to have the TV on when he fell asleep. To top it off, he snored. A real pain in the ass.

Actually, though, I got a decent night's sleep the night before the Super Bowl. When I got up, I remember sitting in the room watching ESPN run back highlights of all the other Super Bowls. And I remember thinking, One day I'm going to be in one of these. I'll sit there and watch our game.

That was kind of cool.

I didn't go to chapel that day. I could talk about superstitions for hours, but one of mine was that I didn't go to chapel for late games, and this one started at 3 p.m., West Coast time. I just hung out in the room until the pre-game meal and our short meeting. Then a bunch of us, who always went to the stadium early, jumped in a couple of cabs. There were Benson, Godfrey, Simms, Phil McConkey, Zeke Mowatt, and me.

We always got to the stadium super-early, like four hours before the game. I didn't like rushing around and having a lot of people in my way when I was getting ready. I liked to get my mind on the game.

We wanted to treat this as normally as possible. Otherwise, you could drive yourself crazy. It might be the Super Bowl, but it's the same rules, same field, same referees. So you want to play the same type of game and not get overly hyped up.

Then it was game time.

When Bill left the Giants in 1991 after winning Super Bowl XXV, somebody asked him if he had one special memory or one special moment. And he said, "Yeah, it's standing in the tunnel at the Rose Bowl, just before they introduce the lineups.

And you know it's you and your guys and you're going out to get the job done."

Maybe, but I don't remember it. I have no idea if they introduced the offense or the defense. To tell the truth, the whole day is a fog to me. I'm not one to remember games. Once I've played them I pretty much put them out of my mind.

Even the Super Bowl.

It was sunny, I think. Yeah, it was sunny. At least when the game started. And I know the San Gabriel Mountains rise up right behind the Rose Bowl. At least, that's what I've been told. I never saw them.

The crowd? I never looked in the stands. In every game when we were on defense, I sat on the end of the bench and I never looked at anything.

I'll tell you what I remember and what I've been told. We killed them.

We beat the Denver Broncos, 39–20. Phil Simms, our quarterback, was the Most Valuable Player. He completed a phenomenal 22 of 25 passes for 268 yards and three touchdowns. And our offense ran the ball 38 times for 136 yards and two more scores.

I do remember we were losing at halftime, 10–9. Ron Erhardt, our offensive coordinator, got in front of the team and said, "We're doing everything we want to do. We just aren't putting the ball in the end zone yet."

And that was it. That was the only game I remember the entire year that we did not make one offensive adjustment at halftime, not one single adjustment. Ron went over what they were giving us, and what we were doing. We just had to put the ball in the end zone and I knew we would. We had them right where we wanted them.

It was different for Heidi. She was up in the stands with her mom, her brother, my parents, and two of her closest friends.

"I usually sit in the stands by myself," Heidi said. "So having all the people around me just added to the pressure. We got all the way there and started losing. It was terrible and I was terrified. You come all the way there and you don't want to go home a loser. It's nerve-wracking. I thought we were going to win, but you never know."

Lee Rouson returned the second-half kickoff 22 yards to our own 37-yard line, so we had pretty good field position. But Joe Morris, running to the left outside of Benson's block, came up a yard short on third-and-three.

That's when Bill made the call that turned the game around. On fourth-and-one from our 46, he sneaked Jeff Rutledge, our backup quarterback, onto the punt unit. We lined up, then Jeff ran up under center and checked the defense. We called it "Arapaho" and Jeff had three reads: a play-action pass, an off-tackle run behind me, or a sneak.

I wasn't surprised that Bill called for the fake. Denver wasn't surprised either. They just got blocked. Rutledge called the sneak and my guy Andre Townsend ripped inside towards Jeff. I got just enough of him and we picked up the first down.

Five plays later, Phil threw a 13-yard touchdown pass to Mark Bavaro and the rout was on.

If I remember one play from that game, besides the fake punt, it was a "slant counter special" in the third quarter. That's a play where Godfrey and I got to pull around to the left side and lead Joe Morris through the hole. Godfrey trapped the defensive end and my man, the linebacker, got caught inside.

There was nobody there to block. I've got a picture of it hanging in my basement, me pulling around the corner with Joe Morris running behind me, right on my hip.

Anyway, I went down to block the safety and I put him right on his back. That's the play I remember most because I got to run and hit one of the little suckers. I don't remember who I hit, but I got him good.

That's when I knew we were starting to roll. I wasn't aware of Phil's numbers, or Joe's numbers. But I knew we were starting to have success. Linemen know because they keep moving down field. That's really all you're aware of.

And as we kept moving, you could see the fight going out of Denver. The longer we played, the less fight they had. We were starting to pound them. You could see it in their eyes. And for an offensive lineman, nothing cranks you up for the next play like seeing that look of surrender on the face of the guy lined up across from you.

By the fourth quarter, it was over. Jim Burt, our nose tackle, who had staged a climb over the wall and into the stands at Giants Stadium when we beat the Redskins to win the NFC championship, was walking around with his pads off and his son hoisted up on his shoulders, mugging for any camera he could find.

Harry Carson, who started something of a sports tradition with the "Gatorade Dump" over Bill's head every time we'd win, was sneaking around the bench, dressed in a security guard's yellow jacket, and Madden was up in the CBS booth, diagramming the sneak attack on his electronic "chalkboard."

But I just kept playing. Even when we got the ball back with 2:06 left in the game, and Bill cleared our bench, I kept playing. See, I didn't have a backup. There was nobody to come in for me. So I'm the only guy who played every offensive play of that season, including every offensive play of the Super Bowl.

And then it was over. I shook hands with Rulon Jones, Denver's defensive end who'd lined up against me most of the day, and sprinted for the locker room.

I still didn't get out fast enough. I hung back by the showers, passing around the Vince Lombardi Trophy. It's a beautiful trophy, especially when you've just won it.

Interviews? For an offensive lineman? I don't think anyone talked to me. In fact, every year the NFL staff runs around collecting quotes and typing them up to distribute to the press. There were 18 pages of quotes from the Giants locker room at Super Bowl XXI. I wasn't on any of them.

Maybe a couple of guys asked me how I felt, but nothing big. A lot of other guys had columns in the newspapers back home, but I didn't. There was no "Karl Nelson's View" in anybody's paper.

I was an offensive lineman. I did my job. That's just what you do. You don't become an offensive lineman for the glory or for the notoriety. You block so the running back can look good, or so Phil Simms has time to complete 22 of 25 passes.

Today, people probably know me a hundred times more for being the football player with cancer than they do for being an offensive lineman in the Super Bowl.

Most people forget that I was a pretty damn good ballplayer.

Chapter 3
Growing Up in the Game

The first time I put on pads was when I was 8 years old, growing up in Illinois. I got one of those kiddie sets for Christmas. You know, the little helmet and everything, with the Chicago Bears' logo.

I didn't play any pee-wee or junior football. It wasn't offered in my town. Besides, I wasn't very athletic growing up. The first time I put on pads for real was in eighth grade. That's the first time they offered football at school.

That was back in DeKalb, which is 60 miles straight west of Chicago, in the middle of the cornfields. I lived about five miles outside of town, so I was in the middle of the middle of the cornfields. That's where I had been born on June 14, 1960.

My brother Kevin was the kind of kid who would shoot baskets when it was 20 below with 20 mile-per-hour winds and five inches of snow on the driveway. But you wouldn't get me out for that. No way. When I did go out there in the summer, he'd block nearly every one of my shots, and I'd run back in the house, not wanting to play.

I played sports because, living in the country, you either played or went home with no friends within a one-mile radius.

I was horrible at baseball until one year in Little League when I figured out what was going on and I went from hitting .150 to hitting .400.

I played basketball and at first I wasn't any good at that, either, but I played just because I was big. My first year in high school, I was six feet tall and the seventh man on the freshman team. That summer, I started blocking my brother's shots out in the driveway.

My sophomore year, I was six feet four inches and starting on the varsity halfway through the year. The four inches had something to do with it, but I was also advancing athletically.

When they moved me up, I was surprised. But Fred Hardman, the varsity coach, had brought up another sophomore at the start of the season, so it wasn't a total shock.

My first varsity game was against East Aurora, and I played against this big black guy. Well, he was big, but I was bigger. Only I had no upper body and he was an animal. The very first play—wham!—he smacked me in the chest with his elbow. He got caught, yeah, but it was a classic intimidation move, like "Welcome, sophomore." I was too stupid to know the difference, though. I kept on playing.

Basketball is really the sport at which I excelled. For me, it required more discipline than football. I think I learned more about hard work and dedication from basketball than football. I was always more challenged there. In the back of my mind, when I think of working hard, it is always at basketball practice.

It's where I learned to do what I was told, also. To bitch about it, yes, but to do it and never question it. That's something I used later in my fight with cancer.

Coach Hardman tried to instill some things about sports in all of us. He'd tell us there are certain people who are going to fight through problems and certain ones who aren't. Basically, that's what sports does—presents you with problems. Every play is a challenge and a chance to fight through it.

I probably got more of that from basketball than football. Football came so late to me, and not seriously until my senior year.

I started football in eighth grade. I was five feet, eight inches, which is bigger than most kids, so I was a tight end and defensive tackle, just because of my size.

As a freshman, I started at defensive end and was a backup offensive lineman. One day when we scrimmaged the sophomores, I was lined up against my brother, and he killed me.

By my junior year, I still wasn't big enough for the offensive line, so I moved back to tight end. But the next year, we got a new coach, Dick Russell.

There wasn't a focused football program at DeKalb until this guy came. We just kind of played and got our asses beat because we were the smallest school in our conference. But Russell brought an intensity to the game and I picked it up.

He's the one who really turned me into a football player. I was six feet six inches and 215 pounds going into my senior year. He pulled me aside the day they handed out the gear that season and said, "Listen, I think you've got size potential.

You've got very little upper–body strength, but if you ever grow into your legs, you're going to be big. I think you can go to any college you want and play football."

Until he said that, I had always thought I would be going to college to play basketball, because I was turning into a pretty good player there.

But I was never a person who thought I was a great player, so I was shocked when this coach started telling me this stuff. I was even more shocked when college recruiters came and started offering me scholarships to big schools.

Our other coaches hadn't really pushed any kids or written to any schools. Coach Russell wrote to over 150 schools about me and all of a sudden I started getting letters from Michigan, Nebraska, and Notre Dame. I was filling out forms and having college coaches come in to talk to me. If it hadn't been for Coach Russell, I would have been playing college basketball somewhere.

I don't really remember the first day of practice that year. My main memory of it is of Coach Russell pulling me aside and telling me, "You're wasted at tight end. You could probably be a good one, but you're not fast enough. So I'll sacrifice that to have you play tackle, because that's where you can play in college."

If winning football games was the only thing he had on his mind, he probably would have left me at tight end, where I would probably have had more direct impact on our games. I think most coaches would have. But he made that switch because he knew it was best for me.

"When you make the pros," he said, "just remember who did this."

When Coach Russell made that crack about the NFL, I thought it was as big a joke as everyone else. The main reason I listened was because he said, "I can get you to a bigger school." I couldn't have played Division I basketball, but I could play Division I football.

He saw something more in me. He even kidded me and said, "I want one percent of your signing bonus." I guess I still owe him that.

I don't remember any of our offense, any of our plays. I do remember once, during practice, breaking a guy's face mask in a tackling drill. All of a sudden practice just stopped and everyone stared.

Another time, we were doing a drill on the seven-man sled.

Coach Russell had told us that if anybody on the team could break one of the padded suspension arms on the sled, he'd buy the guy a steak dinner. So we were doing a drill where you hit the sled and roll to the next pad, hit it and roll, hit it and roll. And I went through the drill and broke two out of the four pads I hit. That shocked the hell out of me. I mean, no one had broken one before and no one did for the rest of the season.

Come to think of it, I never got the dinners. So I guess that's Coach Russell's one percent.

He got me excited about football, for what it could do for me and for what it was. He was a crazy, crazy man. The other coaches we'd had were all pretty laid back, but he let me see an intensity that I hadn't seen before.

He pushed the right buttons. He was a motivator and he really brought the team together. We always had some kind of pre-game meal together. We were always doing things together. That had been unheard of at DeKalb before then.

He was a good coach, and I was a good soldier. As I said, I always tried to do what I was told. I was always very coachable, all the way through. If they said, "Try this," I tried it.

I was brought up to respect and listen to authority figures and not to question them. And that's what I did.

I was in the honor society and played three sports. I guess I was the typical model student. That came from my parents. They instilled those values in me. I was good in school, but I worked at it pretty hard. I wasn't a natural student who didn't have to study, but I always enjoyed studying. I never put up a fuss about having to put in the time. I'd go to practice and as soon as I got home, I'd open up the books. Maybe living out in the country with nothing else to do helped.

Through high school, I was a good student. I got two B's in high school—in typing and second-year Spanish—and the rest were A's.

By the time basketball season came around my senior year, I had already signed with Iowa State. College recruiters would come looking at another kid on our team and want to talk to me, but I was already committed to football.

I could have gone anywhere in the Big 10. And Oklahoma was the only school that didn't recruit me in the Big 8. I even got a letter from USC, but that was for an academic scholarship.

I went on four recruiting visits to Illinois, Northwestern, Oklahoma State, and Iowa State. I remember Michigan was mad at me because I didn't take a visit. I just thought it was a football factory and I would get lost there. I also canceled a trip to Purdue, because I'd already made up my mind and didn't want to waste their time or mine.

Jimmy Johnson, who coached the Dallas Cowboys to a win in Super Bowl XXVII, was at Oklahoma State then. One of his assistants, Donny Deke Pollard, told me, "You'll be starting your freshman year." I think they'd told everybody that, but they even had the president of an oil company call me and promise me a summer job.

That's how some of the schools work, but my parents both went to Iowa State so it wasn't a real tough sell. They never pushed me to go there, but it had everything I wanted, including a great engineering school and a football team that had been 8–3 in each of the preceding two seasons.

Coaches at other schools had promised more. Earle Bruce, who was then at Iowa State, promised a clean program with no probations. His big thing was he'd give you five bucks if you made the dean's list. He'd say, "That's the only thing the NCAA can get me for."

Coach Bruce was there for my first year at Iowa State, when I sat out as a redshirt. That's what the NCAA calls it when you practice with the team but you don't play in the games, so you can retain the year of eligibility.

I didn't really mind that. When I signed my letter of intent to go to Iowa State I weighed 215 pounds. I got up to 242, but after two weeks of two-a-day practices, I was back down to 220. I knew I wasn't big enough to play and I needed that year.

And once again, I went with the company line. Even in college, I didn't question authority. If the coach said get up 5:30 a.m. and be here by 6 a.m. ready to lift, and it was 25 degrees below with a windchill of 75 degrees below, I was still there, I still did it.

The company line my first year was that this was a good year to learn, and it would give me a good start. I was studying engineering and not having to play took the pressure off me my first year. I had had a 3.85 grade point average in high school. My first quarter at Iowa State I had a 2.44 and I thought that was pretty good. I was taking chemistry, physics, calculus, freshman engineering and English, which was my worst subject.

After my first year, Coach Bruce left to go to Ohio State and they brought in Donnie Duncan, who had been an assistant at Oklahoma. When practice started, I was having problems with my back. I had pulled a muscle in high school, and it didn't bother me my redshirt year. But it started acting up the fall of my second year there.

I had to miss a couple of practices and there was a senior who started the first game ahead of me. But he got hurt in the first quarter and I started the next 43 straight games to finish out my college career.

I started them all, but it wasn't that easy. My back went into spasms and felt just horrible a lot of time. I would play on Saturday, then do nothing Sunday, Monday, and Tuesday. By Wednesday, maybe, I'd practice, then again on Thursday. Friday was a light day, then it'd start all over again.

I'd tape my back every game, but that wasn't enough. At halftime of every home game, they'd take me straight to the trainer's room. I never once made it to the meetings where the offensive team put in its adjustments. I wouldn't even know how they ran them. Someone just gave me a quick breakdown of what they'd said and what changes we were making.

While they were working on x's and o's, the trainers were working on my back. I'd get an ice massage for 10 minutes. Then they'd tape my back up and rush me back to the field. If we got the ball back at the start of the half, I'd generally miss the first couple of plays. If we were on defense first, I'd be right on time.

That's what it was like for my sophomore and junior seasons. My back kept me out of spring practice in my junior year, and I thought that was going to be it. I'd already seen five or six orthopedic guys and they never really found anything. Then I started seeing a chiropractor during my senior year. That really kept me going.

Don't ask why I did it, through all that pain. I was a starter, and I guess I was doing my job.

I was the best lineman we had every year after my freshman year. I won an award for that three years in a row. So I knew I had to play, had to fight through the pain. As a player, you just don't question it.

I had to play for me, and for the team, too. I was very team-oriented. I knew if I didn't, I'd be letting the guys down. That's instilled in you in football, especially in the offensive line.

I never saw myself as a great athlete. I saw myself as less than I really was, but I saw myself as part of the team.

I absolutely think that being part of a football team translated to my fight with cancer very well. In football, you've got all these coaches telling you what to do, even though you're the one that actually does it. You're still part of a team and you've got to get your direction. In fighting cancer it's the same, with the doctors telling you what to do and you being the one to do it.

I never had a serious injury until my problems with my back in college. But I never missed a game. I played in 44 in a row, every game through four seasons.

To be an athlete, you have to have the belief that you're indestructible. You have to think it's cool to go out on the field and later have to scrape yourself off the turf just to get back up to the huddle and hear the call for the next play. Then you do it again. That's just what you do.

As long as you're not going to do permanent damage to yourself, I don't think this belief is a horrible thing. It instilled in me a lot of very good values that I've been able to take with me through life. It helped me a lot when I was going through cancer treatment. It enabled me to fight through things on days when I'd feel horrible. I even kept working out all the time I was going through the treatments—the radiation and the chemotherapy both. On days when I felt good enough I'd go down to the stadium, just to keep that attitude.

I saw my treatments as training camp. It's something nobody wants to go through, but something you have to go through to get where you want to be. If you want to play a regular season football game, then play in the playoffs and get to the Super Bowl, you've got to go through training camp.

Treatments and training camp meant going through something I didn't want to go through to get someplace I wanted to be.

Still, it's hard knowing your back is going to be screwed up and you'll have nights when you have to lie on your back with your legs up on a chair because it's the only way to keep your back from going into spasms so you can get to sleep. Or choosing which class you'll go to because you can't sit through two of them back-to-back.

So when I first started getting inquiries about playing professional football, and teams sent questionnaires that you'd fill out and send back, I wrote "I don't know that I want to play professional football."

Honestly, I thought I'd had enough, enough of the pain. And enough, almost, of football. I was tired of it, tired of being cheap labor. Once we figured out that if you added up tuition, room and board, and books—the "salary" of a college athlete— and divided it by the time we spent in meetings and at practice, it came to about 50 cents an hour.

Besides that, I didn't like the way the program was being run. Coach Duncan had come in from Oklahoma where they'd just baby-sit kids who were great players, trying to keep them out of trouble. When he came to Iowa State, he tried to do the same. But he just couldn't get the same caliber of athlete, even though he tried.

They brought in a kid from Chicago who couldn't read. They kept him eligible for a year and a half, then sent him back no better off than when he had arrived. They also had double and triple standards. Running backs could get away with things that offensive linemen couldn't. Of course, offensive linemen didn't get into as much trouble as running backs.

They just didn't run the program the way I thought it should be run. But I never rebelled. That's not my nature, remember.

Finally, Coach Duncan sat me down in the spring of my junior year and said, "I think you can play professional football."

It was just what Coach Russell used to tell me. But I wasn't sure that I wanted to. My back was killing me, I was getting an engineering degree, and I was tired of people using me for my body. I wanted somebody to pay me for my mind.

Then he told me how much I could make playing professional football—about $75,000 to $100,000—which was about three times what I'd be making as an engineer.

I said, "Okay, if they want to do that, they can pay me for my body, and my mind will still be here."

That was the first time I thought seriously about playing pro football.

I was invited to the NFL's scouting combines, the meat market where professional football buys its prime beef. They bring in 300 of the top college players to one site and all the teams get to check them out, firsthand. It's very degrading. They poked and prodded the hell out of me—again, good training for what I had to put up with later.

They really looked hard at me because I had gotten treatment constantly at Iowa State. After all, I was how they justified the ice machine in the trainer's room. I used about 10 pounds a day on my back and my knees, and the book the trainers kept to track my treatments was really thick. I had tendinitis in my knees, so the NFL X-rayed my knees and my back. I remember they sent me to a room that was just about glowing because the guy was taking so many X-rays, and we were joking about the radioactive water all over the floor.

But I didn't have any major injuries other than my back, and I'd still played every game with that. I expected to be drafted, somewhere in the second or third rounds. There were a group of five or six linemen paired up together at the combine, and we were all rated about the same. On draft day, I took the day off from class and sat around in my apartment with six of my friends. I still remember one guy telling me, "Know what? You're going to be the highest–paid graduate out of Iowa State this year. Out of all doctors, lawyers, whatever, you'll have the highest starting salary." I guess I hadn't thought of it like that before.

I watched the draft on ESPN, and all these guys were going late in the first round, then early in the second round. Then everybody stopped taking offensive linemen until the Giants made me their second pick of the third round.

Nobody on the Giants had said they were going to take me. I remember Rosey Brown, their scout, coming out and somebody telling me he was in the Hall of Fame. That impressed me a little, but they had never said they were taking me.

I saw the pick on TV and then I got a call from Vinnie Swerc, one of the Giants' administrative assistants at the time. He said, "Hold on, here's Bill Parcells."

Bill got on the phone and said, "Welcome to the Giants, we're glad to have you here."

And I was thinking, who the heck is this guy?

It was Bill's first year. But I really didn't follow pro football. I didn't know he had just been named head coach, taking over from Ray Perkins.

I didn't even know they played in New Jersey. The first thing I thought when they called my name was, God, I don't want to live in New York. It bothered me, until I got out here and figured out I wouldn't have to.

Anyway, Bill told me I'd have to fly out on Thursday morning, two days after the draft, and I said, "I've got school."

But since I was their property now, I did as I was told and came out for a minicamp. I had been planning to have a party at Iowa State that weekend, and I couldn't even make it. They had the party without me.

I'd also been drafted by the USFL's Tampa Bay Bandits, but when my football agent Jack Mills asked them for a signing bonus, they said, "We were afraid you were going to ask about that." So it was the Giants or nothing.

Growing up, I had thought I was going to be the tallest catcher in major league baseball. Then I thought I'd be a

Division II basketball player. The NFL was not my dream.

For the right money, I'd have gone to the USFL. But it wasn't there. So I headed for the NFL and New Jersey, and Bill Parcells' Giants.

Chapter 4
Indestructible

The very first professional football game I saw live, I played in.

It was the first preseason game of 1983, against the Jets. I was a rookie and I didn't expect to play until late in the game, but somebody had an equipment problem in the second quarter and I went in for the first play of my great pro career.

I totally missed a line call and blocked the wrong guy.

Back in the huddle, guys were asking me, "Didn't you hear the call?"

What call? I didn't hear any call. But Rich Umphrey, the Giants' center, had been screaming at me. We were supposed to do a combination block and I had no clue.

Of course I had no clue who the quarterback was, either. Hey, I'm not even sure it was Giants Stadium.

When I got to my first training camp in the summer of 1983, the Giants had guys like Gordon King, a first-round pick in 1979; Brad Benson, already a six-year veteran; J.T. Turner, in his seventh year; Roy Simmons, Billy Ard, Ernie Hughes, Rich Baldinger, Umphrey.

Kevin Belcher, a sixth-round pick from Texas–El Paso was the only other rookie on the offensive line, and I guess I was intimidated. All the players kept telling me I was going to make the team, but I thought there was no way in hell. I'd go down the roster and say, "I'm not as good as this guy, I'm not as good as that guy."

But they kept telling me I was going to make it. Maybe they just thought the team wouldn't admit a mistake on a third-round choice. Or maybe they saw something, too. But as before, I never thought I was as good as everybody said I was.

If you ask him, Parcells will tell you one story about Karl Nelson and the 1983 camp. He tells everybody about the day that, according to him, I just started crying. Well, I wasn't crying, but I was really whining. My back was bothering me, and that day I had a heat stroke. It's something that happened to me every year in college. My body would just shut down. I'd stop sweating, and once you stop sweating, you're done. I'd black out.

So I got heat stroke, and they led me off the field. But I wasn't crying. I just wasn't mentally ready to play.

Two weeks into camp, I was making a little progress. Then, I got into that first preseason game. There was that first play, when I had no idea of what to do. And again later, in the second half, when the Giants were holding open auditions for spots on their offensive line.

And that's when somebody fell on my foot, and the big toe pulled away from the rest of the toes, tearing ligaments that held it in.

The Giants sent me to a podiatrist in Westwood, New Jersey, where they kept shoving needles between my toes and injecting me with cortisone. I remember Tom Bresnahan, our line coach, saying, "You've got to be ready for next week."

Once the swelling went down, I could walk fine, but I couldn't get up on my toes. None of the veterans believed I was hurt. They all thought it was my back, because they knew I had a history of back trouble.

It was hard. Being a rookie, I felt kind of segregated. Then one day, I was cutting across our practice field at Pace University in Pleasantville, New York, heading up a hill to the cafeteria for lunch. Jimmy Burt, who'd made the team in 1981 as a free agent nose tackle (the toughest way to go in the NFL), yelled something smartass to me. I was just so frustrated I turned around and yelled back, "To hell with you!"

He ran right up to me and said, "You've got to have a thick skin. You can't let anybody mess with your head. You can't let them get to you."

That was very unlike Jimmy, who could be a real pain sometimes. But he got my act straightened out a little bit.

The toe put me on the Injured Reserve list, what everybody calls "IR." That meant I'd be out for the season, though I'd be able to practice when my injury healed. It was just like being a redshirt my first year at Iowa State.

I remember the day they put me on IR. Vinnie Swerc, the administrative assistant, used to be the guy who'd tell players they were cut. "Swerc the Turk" they called him.

He'd knock on a guy's door and say, "The coach wants to see you. Bring your playbook." That was the kiss of death, that "bring your playbook."

So when he knocked on my door, he made sure he said, "Bill wants to see you, but don't bring your playbook." That was nice, because at least I knew what was going on.

I went into Bill's office and sat down. He looked at me and said, "You know who's the best athlete I have on the offensive line?"

I guessed a couple of guys, but he kept shaking his head.

"No," he told me, "it's you. But you weren't able to do anything to show me. I saw you coming on a little bit but now you're hurt and you're not going to be able to help me this year. I've got to put you on IR and I don't want to. I was going to try to carry you through the season, but the doctors say you're going to be out another two or three weeks."

I was out seven to eight weeks, and I would have been ready for the third regular season game, but that didn't make him happy.

"It really ticks me off," he said. "You're the best athlete on my offensive line and I've got to lose you for a year."

In a way, though, it made me feel better. I might have been the best athlete, but I knew I wasn't the best player. And he didn't have to tell me that. I just felt good, because I didn't think he was saying things just to build my confidence. He had no reason to at that point. He must have meant it.

So I was on IR. That was still pretty hard. They kept us off in a separate group, as if torn ligaments and twisted knees were contagious.

Then one day, when the IR guys were off on the side working out, riding stationary bikes and doing rehab work, one of the veterans pointed out that none of the guys who had been on IR in '82—not a single guy—had made the team in '83, at any position. IR, he said, was the kiss of death.

I didn't want that to happen to me. People kept thinking my foot wasn't too bad, but the first time I tried to crank it up, running at three-quarter speed, the toe just flopped around. I had no control over it, and if you can't control your big toe, you have no balance or stability on your feet.

It was two weeks before I could start practicing. I worked hard, just trying to figure out what was going on. That year really helped a lot.

I knew I'd have to learn a lot that year if I was going to play in '84. I knew I was more mentally unprepared than physically unprepared, especially after Parcells told me I had all the tools.

I just had to learn what I was doing, and make sure he couldn't put me into that no-man's land that he keeps for injured players. I tried to get into Bresnahan's head and he really didn't let go of me. He worked with me on my techniques through the year. He'd keep an eye on me and he'd watch film of me when I was out working with the scout squad against the Giants defense.

I was living in an apartment in Westwood, New Jersey. I'd get up in the morning, go to the stadium, come home and cook for myself. Then I'd watch TV and go to bed. My life was nothing but football, and it was lonely.

At practice, I did whatever I could. One day, we were short of defensive linemen in one drill. I hadn't played defense since high school and I had no clue, but I jumped in when Parcells told me to.

Now I was trying. I just wasn't any good on defense. I couldn't do anything right and finally Bill said, "Nelson, get the heck out of there."

I walked back behind the offensive huddle, took my helmet off, slammed it down, and said, "I'm trying my ass off. Don't treat me like that." I was really frustrated, but Bill didn't say a word. He probably didn't even know I was upset.

I don't know if I made any impression. The Giants had plenty of other problems that year, when we finished 3–12–1 under our new coach. And at the end of it, I was thinking, Geez, I'm not even good enough to make this team, a 3–12–1 team.

As usual, I wasn't thinking very highly of myself.

Still, I was confident enough (or dumb enough?) to buy a house that off-season, in the spring of '84.

And then some good things started happening. I started going down to Giants Stadium every day to work with Johnny Parker. Parcells had brought Johnny in from the University of Mississippi to be the Giants' first strength and conditioning coach. He was running a program for six weeks in March and April, so I stayed around New Jersey.

I was working as an engineer at General Automotive Specialty in Carlstadt, New Jersey, but I didn't really like it. It was a boring engineering job, doing time and motion studies. Back then, players weren't making so much money that you wouldn't have to do anything else when you stopped playing.

I planned on retiring before I started playing. That's why I got my degree, that's why I didn't think I'd even play pro football. But I signed my first deal for three years. I didn't have any time frame set. As long as the money was there and I was still enjoying it, I'd play. My dad always said I'd go 10 or 12 years. I always thought a little less.

But I wouldn't have gone anywhere without Parker's program. It really helped a lot. And it kept me in New Jersey.

That's when I met Heidi, so it really paid off.

Some people say Heidi and I are a jigsaw match. I'm a boy from Illinois. She's a real Jersey girl. I'm diplomatic, she's direct. I'm stoic, she wears her heart on her sleeve.

It makes you wonder how we ever got together. Heidi, of course, made the moves.

We met for the first time on St. Patrick's Day in '84 at The Talk of the Town, a dance club in northern New Jersey. A friend of Heidi's wanted to meet a friend of mine, so we all paired up in conversation at the bar. The night grew longer and the hours grew small and I got ready to go.

"Well, it's been nice talking to you," I told her. "I'm going home now."

That got her ticked off. This good-looking blond wasn't used to people not making a fuss over her.

A few weeks later, at the same club, I met her again.

She'd come back to burn me, but we just started talking. And then I was getting ready to leave again. This time, she just asked me to dinner.

We went out the next night to the restaurant Heidi's family owned. That's where she found out I was a football player.

I had seen people making a fuss over the Giants, their local heroes. I didn't like it much, so I told Heidi I was an engineer, which I was.

I didn't lie. I just didn't tell her the whole truth.

Heidi was the best thing that ever happened to me.

When I went to training camp in '84, I felt better about myself. I was better physically and mentally, thanks to Johnny Parker's weight program and Heidi. But I still didn't think I had the team made. And nobody else did, this time either.

We all knew what kind of business the NFL was. J.T. Turner made me realize that.

J.T., as our right guard, lined up next to me on the offensive line. He'd come to the Giants in 1977 as a free agent after a tryout with the Kansas City Chiefs and a season in the defunct World Football League. He had started 88 of the team's last 89 games, including all 16 in '83.

But in '84, he kept telling me he was gone.

I'd say, "But you have great technique, you're better than these guys."

He knew that Bill hated him. J.T. was an older guy, 31 that camp. And he wasn't the best influence. He didn't work very hard in the off-season. He wasn't dedicated to playing football. He'd sit around in the locker room, smoking cigarettes.

I liked him. He was a very interesting guy, good to talk to, and a good player. It was more a matter of off-field problems with Bill than on-field, but that didn't matter. He got cut even though there were three or four other guys who weren't nearly as good who made it. J.T. just didn't fit into Bill's plans for the team. He was gone and Chris Godfrey, who came over from the USFL, took his place.

I was worried enough about my own job. I didn't start out having a very good camp. My technique wasn't very good. I was trying hard, but I wasn't getting it done.

Then one day it just hit me. Bresnahan was trying to get me to keep my head back and away from the defensive man when I was pass blocking. Finally, he just told me, "I don't care if you don't touch another person. I don't care if you don't block a soul. I just want you to keep your head back, all the way back. Put your arms out straight. Try it. I don't care if you don't touch anybody, just try it."

That was kind of like letting go of the rope and trying something new. And it worked.

I was learning the techniques. And I was going to play. Gordon King broke his arm at the end of the '83 season and wasn't ready yet, so the Giants really didn't have another right tackle. I had been brought in to take Benson's spot at left tackle, but with King out I played the right side almost exclusively.

I went into our first preseason game at New England as the starter and I had a great game against the Patriots. I would block my guy, then run down field and make another block to free a receiver for another 10 or 15 yards. I was all over the field that night. It sounds crazy for an offensive lineman to say that, but I was. Bill Belichick, who's now the head coach of the Cleveland Browns, was coaching our linebackers then, and after that game he came up to me and said, "Why didn't you tell us you could play like that?"

Well, nobody had asked.

After that game, I was the starter, and Bill started working on my head. He taught me a lot about how to approach the game mentally.

One day after practice, I was sitting up by the student center at Pace-Pleasantville with Heidi and our dog, a fluffy white Samoyed named Stoli. And along came Parcells.

"Look at you, Nelson," he said, shaking his head. "You got your cute, little, blond wife and your cute, little, white dog. You ain't tough. How can you play in the NFL? You're a wuss!"

The next day, in a goal line drill, some rookie defensive lineman poked me in the eye by accident. I ran down the field after him and told him he'd better not do that again. He was cool, but Lamar Leachman, the defensive line coach, yelled over in his southern drawl, "Get your hands off my boy, Nelson."

I turned to him, and I have no idea why I said this, but I said, "I'll kick your ass, too."

Lamar made sure there were 10 or 20 guys between us, and then started like he was coming after me.

Benson freaked. He was always so worried and he started telling me, "You can't talk to a coach like that! They're going to cut you!"

I ironed things out with Lamar after practice and it was no problem. Then at lunch, I saw Parcells sitting at his usual table, and he said, "Nelson, better watch out. Here comes Lamar."

I just smiled and said, "Hey, we're cool. I just wanted to show you I was tough."

They were pushing me. I had played one preseason game, but that was just one game. They still wanted to see what I had.

Bill was always playing head games. He taught me never to show a defensive lineman your emotion. He ingrained that into me and Heidi hates it, because now I have a hard time showing my emotions. But you can never let the guy across the line know that he's getting to you.

Bill worked on me a lot. He'd get more mad at me for getting mad than for missing a block or screwing up my technique. That's how important he thought it was. He'd say, "I don't give a damn if you miss the block, but I don't want you to let that other guy know that he got the better of you."

On the field, it helped. In the rest of my life? I don't know.

Some people might think a thing like that would help you fight against cancer. If anything, it hurts. Anything you internalize adds stress, and stress is something that will cause problems. Some people—and Heidi is one of them—think that one of the reasons I had my relapse is that I put so much pressure on myself to come back and play, and I kept it all inside. So internalizing emotions can be a negative habit.

Heidi knows that it was a technique Bill taught and it worked for a lot of players. Whether it was helpful to Karl Nelson or not, we just don't know.

Bill really pushed his offensive tackles. He pushed Brad and me harder than the other guys. He knows tackles are the key. You're by yourself out there on the end of the line against the defense's best pass rushers, and that's where the quarterback takes the kill shots. Most of them don't come up the middle. Kill shots come from the outside.

Bill always wanted to make sure his tackles were more prepared than anybody on the team. He'd get to Brad by needling him. But he knew that I wouldn't react the same way. I had my limits. Bill knew he couldn't push me around or bully me. He tried, but he didn't get any reaction, so he got tired of it. I guess he had taught me to hide my emotions a little too well.

But that was at the end of a three-year process. In the summer of '84, I still hadn't shown the Giants anything. How could I? I had been on IR the season before. So they'd gone out and drafted William Roberts, a big kid from Ohio State, with their second first-round pick. They'd taken Conrad Goode, another tackle, from Missouri in the fourth, and David Jordan, a guard from Auburn, in the 10th. And they'd brought in Godfrey, who was a tackle in the USFL. Hey, it's a business, and they were buying insurance.

Once I got the starting job, though, I never let it go. From the first game of 1984 through Super Bowl XXI in January of '87, I played in 55 consecutive games. Hell, I only missed three practices that whole time. I had a lot of sprained ankles and sore knees, and other minor ailments. But it was that "indestructible" mentality that came to my rescue — I believed you just go out and you play. You always know there's a chance you'll get hurt, but you don't think about it, even after it happens.

We had a pretty good season in '84. Our offensive line— Godfrey, Bart Oates, Billy Ard, Brad Benson, and me—really started to come together. We stayed together, as a unit, for practically all of the next three seasons. That's one reason we ended up in the Super Bowl in '87.

We were 9–7 in '84, and would have been better if we hadn't lost our last two games to St. Louis and New Orleans.

But we still got into the playoffs, and headed to California to play the Los Angeles Rams.

During the season, we'd gone out to Anaheim and been embarrassed, 33–12. The worst thing was we'd set an NFL record for giving up three safeties.

I'd had a really awful day against Jack Youngblood, the Rams' 15-year veteran defensive end. He had this move where he'd grab my triceps with his incredibly strong hands. If I was in bad position, he'd just pull by me. If I was in good position, he'd pull me down on top of him and I'd get a holding call.

That was the worst game of my career. Youngblood had three sacks and drew three more holding calls. I didn't directly cause any of those safeties, but I backed us up to our own goal line a couple of times.

So we were playing the Rams in the playoffs, and I had to find a way to stop that one move where he'd grab my arms. I talked to our coaches, I talked to Benson, I talked to everybody. They all said to just lock my arms out and that would do it, but I'd tried that the first time and it hadn't worked.

All I could think about was how to stop that move. It was to be nationally televised, a playoff game. I was scared.

Friday came and I had no idea. Saturday, no idea. Sunday, I was sitting, half-dressed in the trainer's room. I saw a jar on the shelf, and it hit me: Vaseline.

I greased up my upper arms, and on the first pass play, Youngblood grabbed me and slid off with a handful of Vaseline. I had scratch marks all over my arms, but I was still standing. And I had a pretty good game.

Just goes to show that if you can't outfight 'em, outthink 'em.

That was a pretty close game. With about six minutes left, I was blocking my guy and got tripped. He landed right on me, right below my rib cage. Then the pile landed on him.

It pulled two ribs off my rib cage, and they crossed. I was just lying there in agony, my ribs crossed and my legs flopping around. I could hardly breathe.

They took me over to the sidelines and Parcells yells, "Can he go back in?"

Ronnie Barnes, the trainer, shouted back, "We don't know yet."

Parcells says, "I need him. Get him in."

They started to put a flak jacket on me and Parcells looks back again.

"How long?"

"Five minutes."

"There's only five minutes left, I need him now."

Bill was putting Goode in. I saw Burt holding Conrad by the hand, walking him out to the offensive huddle, trying to calm him down.

Conrad finished that series, but I got up and finished the game. We had one more series after that to wrap up the 16–13 win.

While all that was going on in Anaheim, Heidi was back at P.J. Finnegan's, our hangout in Westwood. It's where she went to watch every road game.

She'd gone to the ladies room before I got hurt and when she came out and looked at the television screen, she saw somebody lying on the field.

"Who's that?" she asked.

"Lionel Manuel."

They didn't want Heidi to get upset that I'd been hurt. But she's the type of person who's much better off knowing everything up front. She can handle it if she's got the facts.

And it wasn't too long before she had them. I'm a 6-foot-6, 285–pound, white offensive tackle. Lionel's a 5-foot-11, 175–pound, black receiver.

Heidi was not amused. She didn't go back to Finnegan's for months.

Worse than that, when we won, Bill decided to keep us out in California to get ready for our next playoff game against the San Francisco 49ers. It was supposed to be our first Christmas together and Heidi and I spent it 3,000 miles apart.

We lost that one to the 49ers, who were on their way to winning Super Bowl XIX. I was absolutely miserable, especially when I'd recovered a fumble and everybody piled on, jamming the ball into my ribs.

But it had been a good season. In '83, we had gone 3–12–1. In '84, we were 9–7 and one win in the playoffs. It was a steppingstone. And '85 was another. We went 10–6, with another wild card playoff berth and a playoff win over the 49ers before the Chicago Bears beat us on their way to Super Bowl XX.

That's when we knew we were ready, that it was going to be our turn next.

Coming home on that bitterly cold day in Chicago, we knew we were going to have to work just to get back to where we'd just been. Then we were going to take it a step further.

And we did.

In 1986, the Giants were clearly the best team in the NFL. We had a 14–2 regular season record, including an 11-game roll that carried us into the playoffs. There, we crushed San Francisco, 49–3, and Washington, 17–0.

Then we went out to Pasadena and beat the Denver Broncos, 39–20, in Super Bowl XXI.

In three years, I had started in each and every one of the 55 games the Giants played, including the biggest win of all.

Chapter 5

Super Bowl Fallout

We won Super Bowl XXI, but I didn't get any "top of the world" feeling.

To this day, I haven't even watched the tape of the game all the way through. People used to come over and ask to watch it, and I'd see bits and pieces of it. I know CBS did a close-up on me and I had a drop of sweat hanging on my nose. And John Madden was shouting, "Look at Karl Nelson, the offensive lineman! He's so intense he's got that drop of sweat on his nose and he doesn't care!"

I guess I really ought to sit down sometime and watch it, just to remember what we did, because it was pretty special.

Before I finally announced my retirement from the Giants, I knew I was ready because I started collecting all my old pictures to put up on the walls in my basement. That's when I knew I was done.

It's not that I don't have my memories. I've got plenty of stuff around about the Giants. I just haven't gone back and watched our Super Bowl. I should, but I haven't.

There was that post-game letdown after being so focused on our goal. I felt kind of empty, somehow, once we'd finally reached it.

Our locker room at the Rose Bowl was a zoo, tiny and cramped and crowded. And I didn't get to see Heidi or anybody else until we got back to our hotel, the Westin in Costa Mesa, where we'd stayed earlier in the week.

The game had been over after the third quarter, when we scored 17 unanswered points. But Heidi says, "I was like Karl. I never got crazy. Then, when I wanted to celebrate, I couldn't celebrate. The circumstances were pretty grim."

The Giants didn't really involve the players' families in the celebration. Wives stayed at a different hotel.

"At the Rose Bowl, the wives were told to go right to the buses," Heidi said. "You couldn't meet the players on the way out. You wanted to find your husband, your friends, and hug them and celebrate. And you couldn't."

During the week in California, I roomed with Benson while Heidi and Brittany stayed at their hotel. I had been totally focused on the game, but now that we'd won, I wanted to spend some time with my family.

We had planned on going back to the Westin and having Heidi join me while Benson and his wife got another room. But Brad decided he was going to have a party in our room with his brothers. So we didn't even have a place to stay.

We went downstairs for a while to the Giants' official victory party, but it wasn't a celebration for us. It was like a wedding, and geared to a much older crowd. Most of the players got out of there quickly and partied on their own.

Later, I heard that Sean Landeta, our punter who had a reputation as a real ladies' man, was there with two beautiful blondes. It turns out they were Donna Rice, who was later caught in a scandal with Senator Gary Hart, a presidential candidate, and Marla Maples, who broke up Donald Trump's marriage. But who cared?

We went back upstairs. But we never got a bottle of champagne. "I envisioned winning the Super Bowl and pouring champagne on people, and it just never happened," Heidi said.

We never even got our room. I ended up putting Heidi in a taxi at 4:30 in the morning and she went back to her hotel. But we'd already given her room away, because we thought she'd be staying with me, so she had to sleep on the floor in a friend's room.

The next day, we flew home short on sleep. There were two planes and we had thought the Giants would just let us split up so the guys' wives could be with their husbands, but they didn't. The players went on one plane, the wives and families on another.

The team had a huge pillow fight on the plane. We were grown men, but there was no alcohol allowed and we had to do something to let out our feelings. So we had this pillow fight and I remember Wellington Mara, one of the Giants' co-owners, got hit in the back of the head a few times. But he just flipped 'em back to us so we could keep going.

We came home to a huge snowstorm, and no big celebration. There had been a big ruckus in New York while we were away, with Mayor Ed Koch refusing to recognize us as the city's team because the Maras had moved the franchise to New Jersey in 1976.

The Mets had won the World Series just three months earlier, and Koch made sure they got the ticker-tape parade up Broadway. But he told the Giants if they wanted a parade, we'd have to get one from the mayor of Moonachie, New Jersey, a little town near Giants Stadium.

We ended up with a ceremony at Giants Stadium. We flew back Monday after the game—minus the eight guys who went to Hawaii for the Pro Bowl. The ceremony was set for Tuesday.

Heidi and I woke up that morning, and the radio made it sound like the whole thing was sold out. Traffic was backed up all around the stadium. Heidi didn't even call her family because we thought we'd have trouble getting them in.

When we got there, they put the wives up in the press box and the players on a stage in the middle of the field. It was cold, about 15 degrees, with snow still on the ground. And there were no more than 15,000 people in a stadium that holds 76,000.

"I was really proud when the governor gave you all medals," Heidi said. "But I got more of a feeling when we came home Monday. We took a bus from the airport to our cars, which were parked at the stadium. We got a police escort and the tollkeepers let us go through. When you don't pay a toll in New Jersey, it's a miracle."

I was hoping for more. Honestly, it was pretty disappointing. It looked as if Koch didn't want us and New Jersey didn't want us. It was a shame. Still, I'm not the type of person who expects a big parade. It would have been nice, and we were kind of ticked off that it didn't happen, but that didn't ruin everything for me.

A couple of weeks later, when the guys got back from the Pro Bowl, we were invited to the White House by President Reagan.

Again, I was disappointed. I thought there would be a receiving line, that we'd all shake hands with the President and get a picture of each guy with him. It didn't work that way.

We got to walk around the White House a little bit, then they took us in this room and said, "Stand here. Here comes the President."

We were just in a mass there and he came in, putting his hand out through the crowd to shake ours. He got to everybody, but it was a very impersonal way of doing it. It was definitely, "Wham, bam, thank you ma'am."

Then Harry Carson gave him a jersey, and I've got a picture of that with me in the background.

Reagan, I'm sure, doesn't remember any of it. But when our daughter Lyndsay was born in 1989, just two days after I started chemo treatments, he sent Heidi and me a letter congratulating us and wishing us well. He sent it just before he left office in January of '89, and we've got it framed in our basement.

By the middle of February, the fuss had all pretty much died down. I started working at National Insurance Associates (NIA), an insurance and financial services company, and we found a new house in Montvale, New Jersey. We were anticipating a new contract and a few more years for my career, so we went looking for a bigger place.

We found a place we love, and with some help in design and construction from Heidi's dad and her brothers, and a lot of hard work, we knew we'd have our dream house.

Personally, Heidi and I were on top of the world, with Brittany and our new house. Some people started to recognize me when I'd go out. Giants fans knew who I was, but most people just saw a big guy and wondered if I played any sports. I did some personal appearances, but there weren't as many as I thought there would be.

Giants fans had waited a long time for this. The Giants were great in the 1950s and early '60s and their stars—people like Frank Gifford and Pat Summerall and Sam Huff—really cashed in. Since they were in New York, all the people who ran the advertising industry on Madison Avenue turned them into heroes.

For us, there just wasn't as much demand as everybody had thought there was going to be. Maybe it's because the Mets had just won, or maybe it's because we were in New Jersey.

A few players did cash in. Phil Simms, the Super Bowl MVP, got a few things, like a Disney World spot. Jim Burt, who had staged his act, going over the wall after the NFC championship game at the Meadowlands and then carrying his son around at the Super Bowl, hooked up with a few commercials for trucks and athlete's foot spray. His agent was David Fishof, who also handled Simms and Phil McConkey, and Fishof really pushed it.

Parcells had nicknamed our offensive line, "The Suburbanites" and there was talk of doing a commercial for Suburban wagons, but it never came off.

In fact, there weren't a whole lot of commercials. But there were a lot of books. Simms, Taylor, Burt, Leonard Marshall, and Harry Carson all did books.

But nobody wanted to do "The Karl Nelson Story." So I did a lot of speaking engagements. Mostly, though, I just started to get ready for the next season.

The problem with winning the Super Bowl is that you have to start your off-season program right away or you fall behind everybody else.

So I started going down to the stadium to work out with Johnny Parker. Then we closed on the new house in April and started to move in May.

During the minicamp in May, we got our Super Bowl rings. And that really bothered Heidi.

"The way you got your rings tore my heart out," Heidi said. "We never got to see it. We're what you come home to, we give you a lot of support. We'd like to see you get the award. If your husband was getting an award from some company, you'd get to see him get it. And this was the biggest award they could give."

As a player, something else bothered me. I think there should be only 45 rings, plus enough for the coaches. Frank Gifford has a Super Bowl ring from '86. Why? I think everybody else should get another kind of memento. Something different, something nice. Just something else.

There was a guy, some receiver who had been out all year, whom I hadn't seen since training camp. He was on the sidelines during the Super Bowl. All of a sudden he's part of the team. And he got a ring.

That bothers me. I was the only player who had played every offensive play in 1986 and I got the same thing as the team dentist, the team psychologist, the ticket manager.

Give everybody something. The film crew and the equipment guys and the administrative assistants. You can even give them rings. Just not exactly the same ring. Not the one I'm wearing.

I'm adamant about that. When I'm working in the radio booth now and I hear guys bitchin' and moanin' that they didn't get a ring from the '90 Super Bowl season, I think, Guys, I don't think so.

I didn't get one that year, and it doesn't bother me.

The Super Bowl ring is special. Getting it closed out the '86 season.

For me it was time to move on.

Chapter 6
Cancer

I woke up in the hospital, with Heidi sitting by my bed.

She was holding my hand and, even though I was still groggy from the anesthesia, I could tell she had been crying.

So I looked up at her, and tried to smile. And I said, "Don't worry, I'm going to be fine."

She said, "Are you kidding? Stop it! Karl, you have cancer."

But I'd passed out again.

That was August 20, 1987, but the scene had really started seven months earlier, back in January when we were out at the Super Bowl. I'd been having problems with my left shoulder and Dr. Russ Warren, the Giants' team physician, had checked it out when we were practicing at the Los Angeles Rams facility. He and Ronnie Barnes, our trainer, thought it was just a mild case of tendinitis or bursitis.

It was sore, but it wasn't terrible. It bothered me some during the off-season program when I was lifting, but not enough to make me stop. I kept going from March 15, when we started the program, right through minicamps and up to training camp. It hurt a little more on the bench press and the overhead lifts, but I could handle that.

We opened camp in July of '87, and I started having problems with my shoulder the first week. We came in on Sunday and by the next Saturday I was already missing time because of it. It was really inflamed and the joint was loose, sliding out the back whenever I hit someone.

I tried resting it for two or three days and when I did, I'd get the strength back for a day. The doctors said that when the shoulder got inflamed, the muscles shut down. That's the body's defense mechanism and that's why it got weak. I'd hold my arm straight out and it was so weak that one of our skinny trainers could push it back down with one finger. That isn't good for an offensive lineman, because there's going to be a lot more than just one finger pushing you around.

Parcells started getting mad at me. He told me I had to push myself.

"You've got to know the difference between pain and injury," he said. "If it just hurts, you've got to keep going."

But Russ is a great team doctor. He doesn't put up with any bull from the team. Russ wouldn't make me go unless he knew I couldn't get hurt. He told me I wouldn't get any worse by playing. He just wanted to know if I could still function.

I didn't know. I was missing a lot of time because of it and when I was on the field, I was playing with one arm.

After two weeks of camp, we were getting ready to play in New England for our first exhibition game, our first as the defending Super Bowl champs.

Bill came over to me and said, "I've got to know if I can count on you or not."

So I went out and I played. And after the game, I went over to him in the locker room.

"I played with one arm," I said. "I'm an offensive lineman, and if I'm playing with one arm, at least it's got to be my inside arm, my left arm."

That's where guys beat you. But that's why my arm was bad, because I'd been sticking it out to stop the pass rush, to keep our quarterbacks alive.

Bill just looked at me and said, "I need you. We can't do anything for it now."

I was ticked at him. He was thinking more about how his team needed a right tackle than about me. He wanted me to fight through it and just play. He had done that with Brad Benson's arthritic hip, one he eventually had to have replaced. Brad couldn't get in a stance some days and Bill would tell him, "Shut up and play."

To tell the truth, I was insulted. He was questioning my toughness. Again. I'd played in 55 consecutive games, and had hardly missed a practice, but he was saying I wasn't tough enough.

We almost got into a fight. "I need you," he told me. "I can't have you getting operated on now. You can hold off until the end of the season."

That was six months away!

I knew I was still a damn good ballplayer. I could have made the Pro Bowl with a decent year, but I needed two arms to do that. My body wasn't letting me do what I had to do, but Bill was telling me he couldn't do anything about that now.

I went to Russ and Ronnie and told them I couldn't play. I'd get some quarterback or running back killed. Finally, on the plane home from New England, Ronnie came back to my seat and told me, "We talked Bill into letting you have it scoped. He said you can have the surgery."

I said, "Gee, thanks."

Bill was very angry about my response, which made me angry. Did he really think I liked having my shoulder operated on? I just knew if I was going to play, I needed to have it done, because I couldn't play the way I was.

The plan was to do arthroscopic surgery—that's a "'scope" in NFL language—to try to calm down the inflammation. That might get me through the season. Then, if I needed major surgery, I'd do it when the season was over.

We played New England on Saturday, August 16. The surgery was scheduled for the following Tuesday.

I went in to the Hospital for Special Surgery in New York for my pre-admission tests. I did the blood test, urine, and medical history. Then they said, "We're going to do a chest X-ray."

I said no. I'd just had one in May, as part of the routine physical the players get in minicamp. I didn't think I needed another one.

I said, "It's only August. I had one three months ago. I don't need another chest X-ray now."

But they said, "Hospital rules. You have to have it."

So I said okay.

That night, Heidi brought me a rack of ribs from Rusty's, the restaurant on 73rd Street and Third Avenue, around the corner from the hospital. The restaurant was owned by Rusty Staub, the ex-baseball player who is a Mets' broadcaster now. I wanted to make sure I had a good "last meal" in case anything happened. And have you ever had Rusty's ribs? They're the best.

Russ had already been in that day and told me, "We've got to put this off. They found something on your X-ray."

I'd had a couple of routine X-rays as part of my pre-camp physicals, and they kept finding this spot in my chest. I even went back one time for a CAT scan, but it always turned out to be nothing. So I was very unconcerned. They had found that spot two other times. I thought it was the same stupid thing, which was no big deal.

We had just won a Super Bowl and everything in my life was going great. My shoulder was bothering me, but that's what we were here to fix, right? I was getting ready to have a Pro Bowl year and I wasn't worried.

But Heidi was.

"I came in with the ribs around five o'clock," she says, "and I thought Karl was having a shoulder operation. Jay Goldberg, who is Karl's agent now, was visiting and I was about to leave. Then Karl said, 'By the way, they're not going to do surgery tomorrow. They found a spot on the X-ray and they want to do more tests.' That was the third time, so I knew it was serious. When they find something three times, it's going to be something. And we walked out, Jay and I. Then I saw Dr. Warren there, talking to another specialist."

On Wednesday, Heidi got back to the hospital at 9:30 a.m. and spent the whole day in Russ' waiting room while I saw a bunch of doctors. I had no idea who the hell they were. And I started wondering what are these guys doing? What's the big deal?

Then Russ told me about the surgery. I wanted my shoulder done first, but he said he had to wait. I wanted to know how long. He said he'd just have to wait and see.

Russ brought Heidi into his office and told her he didn't see any need for her to be there the next day. When I came out of surgery, he would call her, and then that would be enough time for her to get back to the hospital.

The next day, the minute I got out of surgery, Russ called Heidi. It was four o'clock on Thursday, August 20, 1987.

Russ told her I had cancer.

They weren't sure what kind yet, but there was a tumor.

Heidi got there just as they were wheeling me up to my room. I was still out, but nobody had told her I'd been out since the surgery.

"I assumed when I saw him that he already knew," Heidi says. "That's why I started to cry. And then he woke up and said, 'Don't worry, I'm going to be fine.' I thought they had already told him and he was just being Karl. Two hours had passed. As soon as I told Karl, I realized he didn't know yet. I thought it was the worst thing I could have done. Thank God he was so groggy he didn't hear me."

I was the last to know. While I was being wheeled

underground across the street to New York Hospital, where they'd perform the exploratory operation called a thoracotomy, the rumor had spread.

I had Hodgkin's Disease. They all knew from that X-ray—a classic. Karl Nelson of the Giants had cancer.

But I didn't know for two more days. See, I had never asked what kind of surgery they were doing. They just said they were going to take a little piece of what was in my chest. I had no idea what kind of surgery I was having, or what they were going to do to me.

Remember, I was a football player. A good soldier. I did what I was told. And I didn't question authority. Especially not doctors. After all, doctors take care of you.

I just wanted to make sure they avoided cutting as much muscle tissue as they possibly could. I was worried about playing again, but I don't remember them shaving me or doing any kind of prep work. I guess they did, but I just shut it out of my head. I trusted that the doctors knew what they were doing. And that was enough.

When I found out what they had done to me, I said, "Yikes!" They had cut my chest from four inches below my arm pit around toward the back, following under the shoulder blade. They had taken out a five-inch piece of rib, collapsed a lung and put in a chest tube. Then they had taken out a small piece of the mass in my chest.

I had thought it was going to be a two–inch cut. But they didn't want to go between my ribs from the front. They already knew they were going to treat me with radiation, and were planning ahead for that.

They told me afterwards that a thoracotomy is one of the more painful surgeries there is. I found out that they were right. But I still remember being amazed when I woke up and there was a tube coming out of my chest.

"What the hell is this?" I asked.

For the next couple of days, I don't remember anybody saying "cancer." Heidi had told me when I first came out of the anesthesia, but I just don't remember it. Everyone else kept calling it a "mass." Not cancer, just "a mass."

Dr. Wolf is the first one I remember saying "cancer." That was on Saturday, August 22, when the Giants were getting ready to play the Cleveland Browns in our second exhibition game.

He came in and said, "You have lymphoma."

I didn't know what that was.

He said, "It's a form of cancer, but it's treatable. You have Hodgkin's Disease, which is the most treatable type of lymphoma there is. You're very lucky. Hodgkin's has a 90–percent cure rate."

I just said, "Okay, what do I have to do to play football again?"

Heidi didn't blink. "I was trying to humor you," she said, "because that's what I thought it would take to get you through it."

And while I was getting the bad news, Bill Parcells was giving it to the Giants in the locker room after they had beaten Cleveland, 24–10.

Which meant that on Sunday, I was the lead story in every newspaper in New York and on every local TV station. That was kind of weird, in an interesting way. I'd turn on the news and I'd find out how I was supposed to be doing and what I could expect. I was getting my Andy Warhol 15 minutes of fame, and I was getting it every night.

I didn't mind, though, because I wasn't trying to hide anything. Brittany, who was two at the time, knew everything. Heidi brought her to the hospital as often as she could.

But security was tight because the Giants wanted it that way.

George Young, the Giants general manager, had called Heidi and told her not to talk to anybody.

"I don't want to fight about this," she told him, "but I grew up here and I have a lot of family and friends here. And I have the right to tell anybody I want to tell."

It was even worse for my second surgery. Then George called Heidi and told her, "We'll call you when we know anything." That went over real big with her.

But Dr. Warren straightened that out. He told George, "It isn't any of your business. His wife will be the first one I'll call."

"The Giants were good to us," Heidi said. "They sent a limo for me every day to take me to the hospital. Maybe they weren't used to wives acting the way I did. They probably didn't know how to handle somebody like me. But I'm not somebody's little girl. That's not their problem. That's Karl's problem. He married me."

No one from the media got through to the hospital, but every reporter who had my number called the house. Heidi wasn't there either and our answering machine just got filled up from nine in the morning to nine-thirty at night.

I was in the hospital for seven days recovering from the

thoracotomy, getting out on August 27. None of my teammates had come to visit me, nobody from the Giants had been by. I guess some of them were in shock. And they were pretty busy in training camp. They just didn't have time.

When I left the hospital, Dr. Wolf told me, "You're going to be treated with radiation. I want you to start storing your sperm." And we were over at the sperm bank when we got another call from him.

"Listen," he said, "we want to do another surgery to determine what stage your cancer is before starting the radiation treatment."

"What this time?" I asked.

"A laparotomy," he said.

This time we asked a few more questions, so we knew how much they were going to cut. Again, I wanted to cut the least muscle tissue possible.

I had just gotten out of the hospital Thursday, and the Giants played their third preseason game that Saturday, losing to the Jets, 30–23, at Giants Stadium. I was back in the hospital three days later, on September 1, for the laparotomy.

This time, I had Rusty's ribs delivered.

When I woke up, the shock this time was that they had stapled me shut. Instead of sewn stitches, I had staples up and down my stomach from where they had cut me at the base of my ribs straight down through the navel to about three inches below the belly button.

They were "staging" me. The surgery was all exploratory. If they had found anything below the diaphragm, they wouldn't have treated me with radiation, but rather with chemotherapy. So they biopsied a little piece of the organs—the kidney, the liver, the lymph nodes up and down the abdominal area—and tested them. They took out the entire spleen, because it is a type of organ that if you take a piece of it, you will destroy all of it. The procedure is called a splenectomy. They were going to radiate the area anyway, and that would've killed it, so they just took it out.

The first day, I was in so much pain that I was asking for painkillers. That's the only time I did that.

I couldn't eat any solid foods for six days, and couldn't drink any liquids, either. I got ice chips and lemon swabs to keep my mouth moist and I had an IV tube to keep me hydrated.

By this time, the Giants had broken camp in Pleasantville

and my teammates were able to come by to visit. George Martin came by, and Chris Godfrey.

Heidi's mother and brothers visited, and some of our friends. Jay Goldberg, who wasn't my agent yet, came by every day with the newspaper and he brought cookies, even though I couldn't eat them. But Steve Rosner, who was the agent who handled my speaking engagements, never even called.

My family? Right after the second operation, Heidi called my parents.

"I told them it was time to come out from Illinois, because this is pretty serious," she said.

It hadn't bothered me, but it had bothered Heidi. So they flew out. And that set up one huge fight.

It was Sunday, September 5, the day after the Giants finished their exhibition schedule with a 26–20 win in Pittsburgh. And I swear I don't remember any of this, but everyone else does.

Let Heidi tell it:

"Karl's parents arrived and we all went to the hospital to see Karl. His parents were there and I was there. Karl's old roommate was there with his wife. My mom was there and my brother was there, and Brittany, too.

"We were all visiting Karl, not some 'sick' person. They were taking pictures and Karl was lying in bed, talking about the team and plays and football. And Chris Godfrey came in.

"Chris walked in and a few people left to let him talk to Karl. But Karl's dad started talking football with Chris, about games and plays and things. Chris' time was really limited. He hadn't even been home from camp yet and he was rushing. He didn't really get to talk to Karl the way he wanted to. When he got up to leave, I just blew up!

"I started yelling at Karl's father, 'This is ridiculous! Karl has cancer! Who gives a damn about football and the Giants and when he's coming back to play!'

"And I stormed out to this sitting area on the roof of the hospital, and I stayed there the rest of the day. When Chris left, I apologized to him. I said, 'I know this isn't the visit you wanted to have.' He gave me a big hug, and said 'I understand.'"

Chris was my best friend on the team. When I first met him in training camp in '84 when he'd come over from the USFL, I'd thought he was a little strange. But once I got to know him, I liked him. He'd come over to our house and do some work, really pitch in. He'd work his ass off and then he'd eat us out of house and home.

That Sunday, he'd come by. Then Fred Hoaglin, who had been my line coach since 1985, stopped by. When he came, my mom got my dad to leave the room so we could talk about a little more than football.

Truthfully, I wasn't up for so many visitors. I'd had two major surgeries in eight days and I can't tell you how painful it was just to cough. I'd turn green and have to hold a pillow to my stomach. But I had to clear my lungs, especially after having one lung collapsed during one of the procedures.

I was just worried about getting back to the team. I really thought I would be out for something like two months, and I was planning on playing toward the end of the season. That is, until they told me that the treatments would last at least that long.

Three days after I got out of the hospital after the laparotomy, I went out to practice. It was just a few days before the Giants were going to open the season in Chicago.

When I parked in the player's lot, the team was already out on the grass practice field next to the stadium, so I went straight out there. After the surgeries, I couldn't really eat. I was down to about 258 from a playing weight of 285 and a lot of guys were scared when they saw me.

That's the way football players are. Nobody wants to see anybody hurt. It's the "indestructible" thing. Everybody wants to see themselves as indestructible. So you never want to associate with someone who isn't healthy.

Heidi couldn't understand. She figured that after I'd blocked my butt off for Phil Simms, we'd have this special kind of camaraderie. It's just not that way. It's a weird business and I don't know that she ever truly appreciated that. Things go on that you just can't explain to an outsider.

She was more impressed by Susan King. After all, the Kings had been the most affected when I took the starting job at right tackle. That had been Gordon King's job.

Gordon was hurt in 1984, the year I came on to win the starting job. But he came back in '85. And I can remember before that season, when we were at the opening of Brad Benson's new car dealership, Brad's wife cornered Heidi and said, "You know, Karl's got Gordon's job. As soon as he comes back, he'll be the starter."

In our minds, there was no doubt it was my job now. The team still had a lot of old cliques, and that would have to change. Back then, though, the other wives were just watching out for their friends, the Kings.

Gordon and Susan never said anything about it, though. And when I got sick, the Kings were some of the people who were kindest to us. Susan King would come to our house and watch Brittany, and cook dinner for us. Gordon would take me for treatments.

Maybe it's because I was a lineman and he was a lineman. When I first walked back after the surgeries, the linemen all talked to me. Some of the other players, though, didn't know what to do.

I don't think Parcells said anything to me at first. Then I remember him talking to me near the trainer's room. He kept telling me, "Anything at all you need, let me know. I'll get it for you. Anything. Anything at all."

In '87, Bill was really weird. He totally withdrew, pulling himself back from the team. He's at his best as a coach when he's communicating with his players, and he stopped doing that. It wasn't real obvious in training camp, but as the year went on he kept pulling further and further away. The NFL Players Association was heading for a strike that year and Bill took it very personally. There were times when I was literally the only player he talked to.

And every day he'd say, "Anything you need?"

He'd ask, "Hey, how you doing, how you handling treatments, what's it like?"

Well, Bill, let me tell you....

Chapter 7

Round 1

The second floor at Memorial Sloan-Kettering Cancer Center has a smell that nobody else seemed to notice. I'd say, "Heidi, don't you smell it?" But she couldn't.

It hit me as soon as I got out of the elevator, like... wham! It didn't smell like anything, really, except to me.

It smelled like radiation treatments to me.

Five times a week, I'd drive my black Chevy S-10 Blazer into Manhattan to Sloan-Kettering, one of the nation's top oncology facilities, and I'd take the elevator up to the second floor.

That's where the radiology unit was. There was one area for people getting X-rays. Farther back was a waiting room for the people getting radiation treatments.

I know I was the healthiest guy in there. At six feet, six inches and 280 pounds, I guess I looked a little out of place.

When my turn came, I'd head into one of the rooms where the radiation machines were set up. I never wore a gown. To me, wearing a gown meant you were sick. And I wasn't sick. I just had Hodgkin's.

I'd just take off my T-shirt, then put my money clip and belt buckle aside. I'd get "cooked," 180 rads at my chest for 35 seconds, then flip over and do the other side.

During treatment, I'd just lie there. A few times, I thought I could smell the radiation, or even smell myself cooking, but there really wasn't an odor. I'd think about the radiation burning out the cancer, but honestly, I didn't feel anything.

Ten minutes later, I was done.

That was the easy part. I had a standing appointment for 9:45 a.m. If I was out of there before 11:30, I considered myself lucky. The waiting was incredible. Some days I didn't get out until one or two o'clock.

I went for my first radiation treatment on September 28, 1987, when Heidi's father drove me in. After that, I went alone. It was just easier, not having to worry about somebody else. I mean, what were they going to do for me? There's already people in there to talk to, so I wasn't alone.

I met some amazing people there. Some of them had burned skin where they had been exposed to intense radiation. Others had to talk through artificial voice boxes. There was one guy who'd drive down from upstate New York, get a dose of radiation in the morning, another in the afternoon, then drive back home at night.

I figured I didn't really have it too bad.

There was plenty of time to get to know everybody. I'd show up for a treatment that was supposed to take 10 or 15 minutes and they'd already know they were an hour and a half behind schedule. Maybe one of the machines would go down and they'd be trying to get twice as many people on one machine. Or there would be emergency patients who would go ahead of you. Something would always back it up.

I'd read, or just talk to people. Some people made a fuss over me because I was an athlete and a New York Giant. It was nice when I got to park for free in a garage near Sloan, but it made me a little uneasy, nonetheless.

I knew people whose skin was crusty from radiation, and people who wore kerchiefs over their necks to cover the holes in their throats. They were dressed in their blue hospital gowns, trying to fight their cancer, yet they remained very dignified.

Everybody thought I was so courageous to fight cancer. Well, it never really took that much courage. The people in the gowns were the brave ones. I was just doing what I had to do.

I had a 90 percent chance of recovery. There was a guy in there, Alex Wallau, who was a boxing analyst for ABC. He had a 20 percent chance. But he was in there fighting every day, and I'm very happy to say he made it.

We'd all trade stories on how we were doing, how we were dealing with side affects. I'd give people tips on high-calorie shakes and high-carbohydrate diets, because radiation sometimes makes it really hard to keep food down.

I became friendly with Tony Boscaino, a cop from Brooklyn. To get through the treatments, we'd joke about them. I'd say, "Tony, how bad are they frying you?" And he'd say, "Karl, where you gettin' zapped today?"

There were different machines set up for different treatments.

Some were set up for the chest, some for the neck. That was a problem for me, though, because of my size. The machines weren't designed to fit people as big as me. They had to set them up about a foot and a half higher, and that changed the physics calculations. It's hard to say one way or the other, but that might be one reason that my Hodgkin's, which is supposed to have a 90-percent cure rate, came back.

Before I had my first radiation session, I had to get "mapped." Four or five days after I was out of the hospital after my second surgery, the laparotomy that set the Hodgkin's at Stage I, they had to grid my body with little tattoos.

I had to lie down on a hard surface for about an hour on my stomach and an hour on my back. But first, it took five minutes just to get me settled down. I was moving very slowly and was very tender, and that table had absolutely no give.

When they got me settled I had to lie still for two hours. They'd put the ink on me, pull the skin back and I'd feel a little prick. It was tedious, and because I was sore from the surgeries, painful.

But that's how they line you up for the radiation. That's how they aim it at just the right spot, which for me was at my chest, neck, and underarms.

They also had to build "lung blocks," thick pieces of metal that they place in front of the radiation unit to keep it from destroying the lungs.

I hadn't talked to the press yet, but the story had gotten out. In fact, it was pretty much a non-story by the time they got to me. It was old news. Throughout the season, all the TV stations came by to do their stories, but I wasn't in the papers every day anymore. And that was fine with me. It had been crazy at our house. Our phone had been ringing off the hook. Fortunately, Heidi's mom and her sister, Donna, were around to handle that, while she tried to take care of me.

And that wasn't easy. I was still playing your dumb jock. I didn't do any research on Hodgkin's. I had doctors telling me that there was a 90-percent cure rate. Why did I need to check that?

Even when I knew it was cancer, I was thinking about football. I knew our season-opener in Chicago was out for me, but I thought I'd come back by the middle of the season. All I could think about was getting back. I was ignoring reality. Heidi brought me back to earth.

She said, "Listen, you have cancer. You're not going to play football this season. Let it go. Let's get you better first. I want a husband, I want a father for Brittany."

That's when I relaxed a little bit and accepted that my season would be totally shot. And I concentrated on the treatments.

They always want to treat you in the least toxic manner possible. If they don't find any cancer below the diaphragm, with Hodgkin's, they can generally treat you with radiation only. After the laparotomy came out clear, showing that there was nothing below the diaphragm, Dr. Wolf told me I'd be treated with radiation, which had a good success rate.

And here's where he went out on a limb for me.

"I'm going to send you over to Sloan," he said.

He was sending me from New York Hospital across the street to Sloan-Kettering. That wasn't the politically correct thing to do, especially with a semifamous patient. But he did it anyway.

Dr. Wolf is a chemotherapist. He was the first oncologist I'd seen. There had been a fight over who would get the case. Wellington Mara, the Giants' co-owner, had his guy and Tim, his nephew and co-owner, had his guy.

Don't get this wrong. Each had my best interests at heart. And I've got to say right here that the Giants were great to me. They paid all the bills. I got private rooms and, if insurance didn't cover it, they paid the difference. They even paid all the deductibles and I didn't know they were going to do that. I ran up a total of $170,000 in bills for the radiation and chemo treatments, and the Giants paid for everything that insurance didn't.

I knew whichever doctor they got for me would be the best. I knew because, basically, I trusted doctors. They were the guys who had always kept me together.

Even during the surgeries, I trusted them, and I'd had some tough times. Like the time I went in for a magnetic resonance imaging (MRI) and I got wedged into the chute.

It was just after the thoracotomy and I was wiped out from the surgery. They brought me down into the sub-basement of New York Hospital and I took one look at the MRI tube and I knew I wasn't going to fit.

It was almost exactly shoulder width for me, but they made me scrunch up my arms and slid me in. I was lying there on the table in that tube, pinned, listening to all the buzzes and clicks and whirs that an MRI makes. I could either lie there and freak out or go to sleep. So I slept, until I heard:

"Mr. Nelson?"

"Yeah?"

"There's a little problem."

"Yeah?"

"You appear to be stuck in the machine."

It took three guys to drag me back out. Then they spun me around and did me feet first.

Then there was the time Dr. Wolf gave me a bone-marrow biopsy. You've got to picture Dr. Wolf—about five feet six inches, in a bow-tie. He came into my room and flipped me over—or I flipped myself over—and he took out this needle that looked like an ice pick.

I was lying on my stomach and gripping the rails at the top of the bed frame. He had to drive the needle through the skin and into the bone to reach the marrow in the middle of my hip. He started jabbing the long needle into each side of my pelvic bone, almost jumping on it to get enough force to pound it in.

I was sweating bullets when I heard him say, "Boy, you've got hard bones."

It was my worst 10 minutes in the hospital. It didn't hurt as bad as knowing that what he was doing was horrible. There is just no way to describe what it was like when he sucked the bone marrow out. It's the most disgusting feeling, because he's literally sucking your insides through a pinhole.

Compared to that, the radiation was nothing.

Of course, there were side effects. Like the way exhaust fumes affected me. Every day when driving the 70 minutes to Sloan-Kettering, I'd head in across the George Washington Bridge and under the apartment buildings on the Manhattan side. I'd smell all the exhaust fumes. I couldn't have the windows and the vents open. I still can't. For some reason, the smell reminded me of the radiation treatments. Maybe it was just psychological, like that smell on the second floor at Sloan, but it made me ill, and it still does.

I also had a problem with my taste buds. My throat was being radiated and that effected me. After my very first treatment, I came home and Heidi had cooked a veal marsala (veal in a wine sauce). I took one bite and said, "Hon, would it be all right if I went down to the Dairy Queen and got a shake?"

Veal marsala wasn't doing it for me. But neither did the shake. The radiation had already screwed up my tastes.

There were other side effects. My hair fell out in a little semi-circle above the neckline, where the radiation was hitting it. And I was tired a lot. I'd always had a problem being light-headed when I stood up, and the radiation made that worse. Once, I passed out in the kitchen and fell over on a little bench that Brittany had. I scraped myself up pretty good.

The radiation also gave me "cotton mouth". It messed up the salivary glands. And because my teeth weren't being cleaned naturally by the saliva, I got a lot of cavities. Now I use a special fluoride rinse for my teeth.

I guess I never really felt sick from the cancer. Just from the treatments.

Soon I settled into a routine. I'd drive into Manhattan for my treatment, and then, if they were done by noon, I'd head over to Giants Stadium to work out.

The guys who knew me well would come up and talk to me. But the other guys would stay away.

It wasn't just an "IR" thing. It was cancer. They were afraid. They were worried that they'd get it, too. Bill and Ronnie Barnes met with some of the players who were having trouble coping. And then the rumors started cropping up.

There had always been stories that Giants Stadium, which is built on landfill in the New Jersey swamps, sits on a load of toxic waste. Harry Carson, who'd played at the stadium since it had opened in 1976, was walking around in a surgical mask and making cracks about not taking showers in radioactive water.

See, I wasn't the first Giants player to get cancer. Dan Lloyd, a linebacker with the Giants for four years, came down with lymphatic cancer in 1980, but recovered. Doug Kotar, a running back, died in 1983 of a brain tumor. And John Tuggle, the running back who was the last pick of the last round of the '83 draft I'd come in, died of cancer in 1986.

Players were wondering if I was going to die and if they were going to be next. And suddenly, there were screaming headlines in the *New York Post* and the *Daily News* about the "Mystery of the Meadowlands."

The result was a $200,000 study by the New Jersey Sports and Exposition Authority, the organization that runs Giants Stadium and the racetrack and arena at the complex. It examined the medical records of everyone ever employed there— almost 10,000 people—and tested air, soil, and water samples.

The study said that there was no conclusive link between the Giants Stadium environment and cancer. But that didn't stop people from worrying. A lot of players went out and had CAT scans done.

They were worried about getting cancer. I already had cancer. I was dealing with that.

When I got sick, people started sending us books and herbal teas and advice on meditation. They meant well, but I didn't read any of it, didn't do any of it. All that stuff does is tell you to keep a positive mental attitude and I had already learned that through football. I knew how to fight through problems.

Between my two surgeries, Jay Goldberg, who's my agent now, hooked me up with Jeff Blatnick. Jeff had Hodgkin's in '82 and came back to win a gold medal in wrestling in the '84 Olympics in Los Angeles. It was real good for me to be able to talk to somebody who was a world-class athlete and had come back. We talked about the radiation and what it did to him. And he told me he'd worked out all through it and didn't have a problem.

Talking to Jeff helped a lot. There are a lot of support groups available, but the one thing that helped me most was to speak with someone who had what I had and not only survived, but made it back to the top of his game.

Of course, everybody reacts differently. Some people get violently ill from radiation, but most people don't. I didn't, except once when I pushed myself too hard. I'd only gotten seven hours of sleep for two or three nights in a row and I was moving some heavy rocks out by our swimming pool. When I went in to take a shower, I just lost it.

But having the house was tremendous. It gave me one more thing to do, something else to focus on. We had bought it just before I got sick and it was something Heidi and I really loved. It took a lot of work, but we loved it.

I had plenty of other things to keep me going, too. When I was in the hospital for my laparotomy, Jay had come in and asked me if I'd be interested in working the Giants' radio broadcasts on WNEW. They were opening the season in Chicago and I wasn't going to be ready to travel, but I was in the booth in time for the second game of the season at home against the Dallas Cowboys.

Then, the NFL Players Association went on strike. I told WNEW I wouldn't work any of the scab games, and they respected that, since I was still a player myself, although not active. And I was still getting paid.

That was a real tough situation. The Giants used to have union meetings in Washington Township, just down the road from our house. I went to one of the first ones, stood up and told everyone, "I apologize to you guys, but the Maras have decided to pay me during the strike. And I'm in a little different situation."

Nobody came up and said, "Hey, Scab." They understood.

But it was still awkward. At one of the scab games, when all the players were picketing out in the parking lot, Heidi and I went down there to be with them. We probably shouldn't have, considering how much the Maras had done for us, but we did anyway. These guys were my teammates, and I wanted to support them.

At least the strike gave me four weekends that year when I didn't have to watch football. And that made it easier. Because it had finally kicked in that my season was done. But so were the Giants. After an 0–2 start with our regular players, the scabs went 0–3. When the strike ended, the team couldn't recover. And, with Bill in a funk, we defended our Super Bowl title with a 6–9 record and missed the playoffs.

The NFLPA strike started September 27. I took my first radiation hit the next day. I got 20 treatments in the mantle area, which is the chest, neck, and underarms. Then I got three "cone-down" treatments, intense blasts to where the mass was first found.

That took five weeks, and originally I had thought that would be it. I had been counting them off. I didn't know that the doctors would wait four or five days until my blood count went up and then give me 20 more on my midsection.

"When they originally told us," Heidi said to me, "they said they were going to do 20 and possibly 20 more. So I figured 40. You figured 20. I don't think I'm pessimistic—just realistic."

It bummed me out, and I was upset.

I had been getting chest X-rays once a week to make sure the mass was shrinking, and it was. Sometimes, though, it was hard to tell. Once, they showed my X-ray to one of the interns.

"This person's still alive?" he asked. "The nodes on his neck are hugely swollen! "

He thought my neck muscles were my nodes. I guess he'd never seen a 19-inch neck before.

But the mass was shrinking and I didn't want to do any more than I had to. I told them, "You didn't find anything below my stomach—why do you have to do anything down here?" They said, "This is a precaution, this is what we do."

Remember, I always listened to the doctors. Heidi says I was a real "hurt puppy" for three or four days, and I was. But I took the next 20 to my stomach.

And I started counting down again. Only this time, I was a little cautious. I didn't know when they were going to pop in and say, "We just need to do a little more."

Finally, I finished up on December 9. I didn't do anything special after that last treatment. I went in and came back out, said a few goodbyes. But I knew I'd be going back for checkups. Then I drove to the stadium to work out.

I worked the Giants game in St. Louis as the third man in the broadcast booth on December 13, and then we took a five-day trip to Disney World. It was the week before Christmas and it was great. The park wasn't crowded and there were no lines. We got a chance to get back to being Karl and Heidi.

I think the treatments were tougher on Heidi than on me. Partly, it's my makeup. Sometimes it's tougher on the people who love you. When you're going through it, you know you can endure. But when it's not you going through it, you don't really know. It's very hard to know how to help somebody, especially someone like me.

I used to give speeches and say, "I always led such a charmed life. I was good in school and good in sports. I got a scholarship and was drafted by the Giants, where I started for three years and won a Super Bowl. And I always knew something bad was going to happen, so if this is the worst thing that happens, I'll feel very lucky."

She hated that. It drove her crazy.

"Every time you said that, I wanted to punch you," she told me. "You had the cancer, but I had to live with the disease. Can you understand that? I was the emotional support. I was the one handling the press, 30 to 50 calls a day. I was 25 years old, and I had a child and a husband who was sick and who didn't want my help, didn't want anybody's help. It was no problem for you, but it's a problem for anyone who's a part of your support system. Nothing bothers Karl Nelson. But I didn't know what to do and I was trying to do it all. You don't relate your feelings. I had to pull things out of you. And you had this 'other' life in a waiting room with all these other people. And I had nothing to do with that."

Part of Heidi's answer was to throw herself into work with the Tomorrows Children's Fund, a charity that helps kids with cancer. To her, the more money she raised for those kids, the more she was helping her husband.

If there were support groups out there, I didn't know about them. Maybe they did tell me about them at the hospital, but

I suppose I would have just ignored them. I talked to Jeff Blatnick and he's the only support group I ever had, the only one I needed.

David Jurist, the president of Tomorrow's Children, later became Heidi's support. He called our house one night and she talked to him for an hour and a half.

"He had the most soothing and calming voice I had ever heard," Heidi said. "He made the most sense to me of anybody I had talked to in a year. And he knew what I was going through. He explained things to me. After that, David would call me almost every day."

I think it's always as hard or harder on the spouse. I'm just glad I was married at the time and had Heidi's support. It would be very tough to handle such a situation as a single. But it depends on the type of person. A very giving person would rather give to somebody else. I'm more of a self-centered person who kept a lot of things inside.

One day, Heidi went on strike. She just got tired of it all. She started walking around holding a wooden spoon like a picket sign. She was tired of cooking and cleaning and doing laundry and dishes.

I think she needed the vacation in Florida more than I did. And it was great. Then we came home and three days later it was Christmas, and I thought the whole thing was pretty much behind me.

I had been everybody's Thanksgiving story. Mike Lupica of the *Daily News* did a big column and I was on the back page of the paper. I was featured on HBO and all the networks. There were so many film crews going through our house that we'd tell them where to set up their lights and cameras. We'd take my big leather chair and put it in front of the fireplace in our family room, and tell them, "Trust us, it's best if you do it this way."

All the local stations came out, and we did CBS, NBC, CNN, ESPN, MSG. One crew came from California to tape a public service announcement for Project Literacy U.S. and I was about two hours late, held up with a treatment in New York. Heidi didn't know what to do to entertain them, so she had them set up all the VCRs in our house. They set all the controls and the clocks, so they weren't blinking "12:00:00" anymore.

By Christmas, things had settled down. But it was going to pick up again.

The Super Bowl didn't make me a star. But cancer did.

Chapter 8
Comeback

I was working out at Giants Stadium in April, when the phone in the weight room rang. The NFL had announced its schedule for the 1988 season, so I knew exactly who it was.

"I've heard, Bill. We open with Washington."

"That's right," Parcells said. "Monday night. National TV. Fifty million fans. It'll be billed as 'The Karl Nelson Comeback Tour.'"

"Yeah, if I screw up, everyone will know."

"Nah, after Charles Mann's first sack, it will seem like you never left."

But I still had a long way to go to get there.

The comeback started, really, after the radiation treatments when I finally went in to have my shoulder operation.

It was the shoulder, remember, that had sent me to the hospital in July of '87, and that led to the discovery of my cancer.

Now that I'd battled through the Hodgkin's, I was ready to move on. And the shoulder was the first order of business.

They had to wait for my blood count to come back up after the radiation and so they set the surgery for sometime after the first of the year.

I went in for the operation on January 5, 1988. I still wasn't sure what I was going to have done to it. In fact, I'm still not sure what was done.

I read about it once, in *Sports Illustrated*. Let me just tell you what they said:

"Nelson underwent innovative, intricate shoulder surgery that may have helped to extend his career. The head of Nelson's left humerus bone had popped out of the back of his shoulder joint, an uncommon dislocation. Warren, a leading shoulder specialist, performed a posterior shoulder stabilization, in which he tightened the joint in Nelson's upper back by repairing the soft tissue of the shoulder and grafting the tissue onto the muscle of his upper back. Warren also removed a piece of shoulder blade that had broken off."

Well, if they say so...

All I know is that when I went in, they weren't sure if they'd just 'scope it, or do a full surgery. They told me, "It depends on what we find. But if we have to do the full surgery, there's a special brace you'll have to wear."

The brace was an orthoplast cast molded to fit around my midsection, and closed with hook and loop tape. There was another cast around my arm to keep it in a bent position, and there were struts to keep the cast in place.

It was a monstrosity, made just for me. And I was praying I wouldn't need it. But when I woke up from surgery, I was in it. And I knew they'd done full surgery.

I was stuck in that brace for six weeks. I couldn't take it off, even to take a shower. I had to have sponge baths, and that wasn't as much fun as it sounds. I used tons of baby powder, but, as they say in the deodorant commercials, I was "malodorous."

I couldn't sleep in a bed, either. The brace was very uncomfortable to lie down in. My hand was sticking out at a 90-degree angle, like I had frozen while shaking hands. And it was really weird for Heidi. Imagine you're in bed, sound asleep, and you wake up and see this person's hand, clenched into a fist, right over you. She could almost envision that clenched fist holding a knife. So I wound up sleeping in a reclining chair.

I spent six weeks in that thing. The day I got out of it, I went straight from Russ's office to the stadium. That was important for me, to start my rehab right away. But it didn't make Heidi too happy.

"I want you to come back," Heidi said. "But first, I want you to be cured. And I want you to have in your mind that your family is more important than football. Your family is supposed to be the most important thing. When you got sick, we weren't. The most important thing was football. And that's why I had a problem with it."

When I'd gotten sick, Heidi straightened me out.

"I'm not going to put up with it," she said. "I'm not going to be second to anything. Either you are going to put Brittany and me first, or I'm going to get out of this marriage."

But after the radiation treatments, she was back to being 100 percent behind me, football and all.

"Not only do I want you to come back," she said, "but I want you to make the Pro Bowl, because I think you got ripped off in the Super Bowl year."

Well, if I was going to do that, I wanted to start right away. And I did.

My grandparents down in Florida had talked to some of their friends who were doctors. They said there was absolutely no way anyone could play football after a thoracotomy and a laparotomy. Then, there was the radiation as a side bonus.

But the cancer and the radiation treatment didn't stop me from playing football. It just took a year away. And then it was too hard to come back with a shoulder that was just a piece of raw meat. And that's what mine was.

The normal recovery time for a shoulder operation like mine was 12 months. I had to get it done in six to be ready for training camp. Then I had to get ready for the start of the regular season, for that "Monday Night" game against Washington.

An offensive lineman either plays or he doesn't. The coach doesn't work you in for a couple of plays the way he does with a running back or a receiver coming off an injury. An offensive line must play as a unit. I needed to be ready for the opener, not the 10th game of the season.

That's why I was so anxious to start. I had a lot to do.

First, I had to stretch my arm out straight again. The ligaments had shortened after being in the brace for so long. That took a few days. Then I started working on getting range of motion back, doing things like running a string over a bar, hand-to-hand, and pulling my arm back and forth with my good right hand. I got trigger-point rubdowns to flush knots out of muscle. They hurt like hell, but I got through it, just like always.

Once I'd worked up a good range of motion, I tied surgical tubing to doors and used it to build up strength in the joint. Then I moved up to light weights, working them up and down and sideways, turning and twisting them at arm's length. And all the time, I'd be riding the stationary bikes, because I had to keep the rest of my body in shape, too. I'd work out with one arm, using 120-pound dumbbells and doing one-armed power cleans.

I'd see Parcells constantly. He'd come over and talk to me about how to mentally prepare myself and what I needed to do.

I know he wanted me to make it, but he wasn't taking any

chances. The Giants used their first two picks in the draft to take Eric Moore, a tackle from Indiana, and John "Jumbo" Elliot, another tackle from Michigan. Hey, it's a business. I understood that. And they'd done it before in '84, when they drafted William Roberts and Conrad Goode and brought in Chris Godfrey from the USFL after I'd spent my first year on Injured Reserve.

I knew what I had to do, and I kept doing it. Mike Ryan, who joined the Giants' training staff in May of '88, kept working with me. I started to work on a Cybex machine for my shoulder, working it up and down and across my body. I'd toss a medicine ball, working on the timing of somebody coming in to hit me. I hit the heavy bag, popping it with straight-arm blocks.

I'd go to the stadium four days a week, for two hours of shoulder rehab, then three hours of lifting. The fifth day, I'd do a couple more hours of rehab.

I don't know that my shoulder would have fully recovered even if I had a full 12 months. Mark Bavaro, our All-Pro tight end, had the same surgery I did and he came back much better. But he didn't have as much arthritis as I did. I think some people's joints are just predisposed to wear and tear, and I think mine are.

My shoulder is the one and only thing that stopped me from having the success I should have had in my comeback. It had nothing to do with Hodgkin's. That didn't slow me down a bit.

In the middle of June, I felt comfortable enough to start running. Two years before, I'd run the Giants' tests—five 220-yard sprints, with a three-to-one rest ratio—all within .12 seconds of each other. My times ranged from 30.05 to 30.17, and that's pretty damn good for an offensive lineman. In '88, I finished my last one in 34 seconds.

Later, when I had tests done before the chemo, the doctors said that the radiation had damaged some tissue in the lungs and they also found some fluid around my heart. So there were some side effects. I guess I wasn't in the same shape, but I was in decent shape.

And that's all I thought I needed. I wasn't planning on playing forever. I thought I'd play two or three more years. With the notoriety I had, I just needed a decent year and I'd make the Pro Bowl. Then maybe a year or two after that, and I'd be out.

What I really wanted was the Pro Bowl. That, and one more contract to pay off the house. Then I could leave.

On July 18, I went to camp. The Giants had moved training camp from Pace University in Pleasantville, New York to Fairleigh Dickinson University in Madison, New Jersey. I was one of just a handful of veterans mixed in with a group of 60 rookies.

When I showed up, I was under the microscope. The first day, I talked to a group of 20 reporters. All that, for an offensive lineman.

"A lot of people have told me that I'm an inspiration," I told them. "But I'm doing this for myself. I just want to get back to being a good offensive lineman... so nobody will talk to me."

I started out working just one of the two practice sessions a day. That gave my left shoulder a little bit of time off. But Parcells made sure I didn't get too much of a rest.

Bill had George Martin and Eric Dorsey, our left defensive ends, attack my left shoulder, giving it the full treatment with their inside techniques. He wanted to see what I had. He had used George as his "weapon" that time in '84 when I'd gotten hurt in the playoff game against the Rams, too, to see if I was ready for the 49ers.

Bill was determined not to give me any sympathy. And he was probably right, I didn't want any.

But I didn't want his head games, either. He was talking to me every day now, really messing with me.

One day, he would tell me I was making good progress. The next day, I was horrible.

Bill told the writers, "I have to find a way to make this thing work. Karl's got this one thing, just one thing, he isn't doing. He knows what it is, but I have to make him do it. It's not his work level, it's his confidence. He's got to believe he can do it. I'm in touch with the doctors all the time and they told me I could push him, so I am. He's mad at me because I get mad at him. But he's not using his left arm and shoulder like he should. That's why I use Martin and Dorsey.

"Do you think I like yelling at him? He's got every excuse for not making it. But he's just got to do it. He's a great kid and he's working hard, but you don't get any gold medals for trying. That's what you're supposed to do. You get gold medals for getting things done."

Bill thought he was giving me what I needed. I don't know if I saw it that way.

As my shoulder got sore, it got weaker. So I couldn't use it.

Russ told Bill I needed a day off, and that really ticked Bill off.

"I just talked to Warren," he told me. "Nelson, you sold me out."

"By getting a day off, Bill?"

"You don't need a day off."

I did, every four or five days. There was still inflammation and my shoulder wasn't working properly. But to keep Bill happy, I took anti-inflammatory medication. I took it until I got an ulcer.

Then one day in camp, Bill came up to me and said, "Karl, you're not progressing the way you should be. I don't think you're going to be a factor on this football team until October."

I just walked away and thought what the hell am I doing here?

That floored me. It rocked me, just crushed me when he told me that. But it was all part of his plan.

Three or four days after he told me I'd be out until October, he was pumping me up about Charles Mann and the Redskins again. And it was like, "Gotcha!"

That's the way it went. Bill loved to ride me. He loved to do it in front of the crowd that comes to watch us practice at training camp. He always had cute little barbs to throw my way.

Bill was always questioning my toughness. He told Joe Morris, "Karl just doesn't seem as tough as he used to be."

Of course, he knew Joe would come right over and tell me.

The next day in practice, I locked up with Dorsey in a one-on-one drill. I pushed him, he pushed me, then I grabbed his facemask and twisted. He started getting all hyped up, but I just told him, "Settle the hell down. I'm just doing this to show Parcells how tough I am."

It was just like when I'd challenged Lamar Leachman to that fight back in '84. But maybe he was right. Maybe I wasn't as tough.

After what I'd been through, though, I didn't think I'd have to prove anything to anybody.

It was hot and cold mind games back and forth. One time I practiced six days in a row and Bill told me it was okay to take a day off.

A little later, he came up and told me it was the fifth time in 10 days I'd had off and that it was too much.

"You're selling me out, Nelson," he told me. "You're not giving me a chance and you're not giving yourself a chance."

But I didn't have the strength. I was worn out from camp, plus doing my shoulder rehab every day. And I got pinched cartilage in my knee. So I had to spend a lot of extra time on my body, time you don't want to spend, especially during camp.

I got a little break because we got a lot of rain. But it was terribly hot. Jumbo Elliot, who'd come to his first NFL camp at 305 pounds, had trainers following him all over the field with water bottles. He kept going down, which meant the lines at tackle were shorter. I had to go 14 plays in a row once because we had no other tackles.

Now throw in one more factor. Heidi was pregnant, and that made her an emotional wreck. She was having a lot of problems with some of the other wives. They resented her because she was able to use my situation to raise a little more money for some of the charities, especially for the Tomorrows Children's Fund.

It was all in the mix when we played our first preseason game in Green Bay on August 6.

I played okay, but I wasn't playing against anybody great.

I started ahead of Elliot and Doug Riesenberg, a second-year guy from the University of California. But something was missing. My intensity wasn't there. I didn't mentally prepare for the game the way I should have. My parents were at the game, and my sister and brother were there. That was a little bit of a distraction. And so many crazy things were going on, with my comeback and everything, that I couldn't concentrate.

Our second game was a week later at home against the Jets. Two days before the game, Parcells, in his daily press conference, had said, "I'm not trying to sound an alarm. Karl's been at it only three weeks and maybe it's going to take five. I don't know what my expectations should be at this time. But I'm going to have to start making contingency plans. I've got to get a right tackle, whether it's Karl or somebody else."

More head games.

I played better against the Jets, in for about 40 plays or about twice as many as I'd been in for against Green Bay. And I helped hold Mark Gastineau, the Jets' glamour-boy defensive end, without a sack.

The next week, Parcells moved Riesenberg from my backup over to the left side. That was supposed to be some kind of signal that I had shown enough progress to satisfy him.

We played our third game against the Pittsburgh Steelers and then closed out our preseason schedule with the Cleveland Browns. Just before we traveled to Ohio for that game, the Giants held their annual kickoff luncheon, a big event every year in Manhattan.

They call out the name of each guy for the crowd and some guys get bigger cheers than others. Lawrence Taylor always gets the biggest cheer, then Phil Simms. But when Jim Gordon, the Giants' radio announcer who emceed the luncheon, said, "Number 63, Karl Nelson," everybody stood up cheering and the whole thing just stopped for about five minutes.

I was standing there next to Godfrey, and I just leaned over and whispered, "Parcells isn't going to let this drop without giving me grief."

Later that night, I saw Parcells in our hotel in Cleveland. And I was waiting for the zinger.

He said, "Karl, you deserve it. It was really a great honor to you and I hope you appreciate what it means to everybody, how much they all want you to come back."

I was a little stunned.

I played our last preseason game against the Browns, and I played a lot better. When it was over, Carl Hairston, their defensive end who had been in our division when he was with the Philadelphia Eagles, came up and said, "Welcome back, glad you're better." And Bubba Baker, who had been with St. Louis and had given me some great battles, said, "Good luck. I hope you make it all the way back."

That was it. Exhibitions were over.

I was ready for showtime.

Chapter 9
Showtime

Lights! Camera! Action!

"Monday Night Football." The Giants and their arch rivals, the Washington Redskins, the defending Super Bowl champs.

September 5, 1988.

Opening night for "The Karl Nelson Comeback Tour."

ABC opened the broadcast with me. Normally, they time it out so their announcers are giving their opening comments as the teams are being introduced. But they came on early and went to a live shot of me, coming out of the tunnel for my introduction and then running to my teammates lined up to greet me on the field.

I was so hyped up, I was in another world. Bob Sheppard, the Giants Stadium announcer, who also works the public address system at Yankee Stadium and has introduced some of the greatest names in sports, said my name and the whole place just stood and cheered. It lasted only three or four minutes, but it seemed like forever.

Heidi was up in the stands, as always. Only this time was special. She was as big a part of my comeback as anyone could have been, and ABC had the cameras on her, too.

"I had chills up and down my body," she told me. "It was the proudest moment of my life. It was something you might imagine happening, but never think it would. Because you're not Lawrence Taylor, you're not Phil Simms."

But that night, I didn't have to be.

The whole day had been too long. If it had been on Sunday, a one o'clock game, I wouldn't have been as pumped up. But all the work and everything I had put in was coming down to this day. And I had all day to sit around and think about it.

I went to the Woodcliff Lake Hilton, where the team always

stayed before home games, then back home for a couple of hours, then back to the hotel. That was so I could drive to the stadium with Benson. It was one of our rituals, our traditions.

I tried not to think about the game, tried just thinking about Charles Mann, the Redskins defensive end, who'd be lined up against me.

I wasn't worried about the cancer, or the radiation treatments. I was thinking about my shoulder, and that I hadn't played in a game (a real game, not an exhibition) in over a year. My last one was Super Bowl XXI, and that had been a long time ago.

We got to the stadium and I tried to do whatever I always did. Just like the Super Bowl, I tried to pretend it was just a normal game. And it was, until the introductions.

I remember I heard my name announced, and I tried to do what I always did, which was to run out and down the line of players, then go over and put my helmet on the bench and practice my pass-blocking sets. And I did that.

Then I noticed that they weren't announcing anybody else. The place was just going nuts! It got me so wound up and crazy that I was worthless. And it showed during the game.

Honestly, I was horrible. I was so wired, I was overreacting to everything Mann did. He's a guy who does a lot of double moves, and that was the worst kind of guy for me to face. I would have been much better off against Reggie White, the great Philadelphia Eagles lineman, who just would have tried to run over me. I might have been able to handle that.

I'm not sure I laid a hand on Mann the first two times he rushed. It was a nightmare.

At halftime, they were going to put Heidi on, but they called that off midway through the second quarter. I can't tell you how relieved she was.

"What could I have said?" she asked me. "That I was so proud of you, even though you were terrible that night?"

At half time, Frank Gifford introduced a feature ABC had taped.

"We told you at the beginning of tonight's show a little bit about the Karl Nelson story... He's struggling tonight, but he's out there. That in itself is a miracle."

After the piece, Gifford came back and said, "Bill Parcells has hassled Karl Nelson, but the other day in a team meeting, when the story of Lawrence Taylor's suspension broke, it was Bill Parcells who called his team together and in an impassioned speech, a locker room speech, said, 'That's not what this game is about. That's not what life is about. What this game is about and what life is about is number 63, the Karl Nelsons of the world.' He's back, he's having a tough time tonight, but Karl Nelson is doing what he loves to do, playing the game of football."

Things were a little rocky for the Giants that night at first. The Redskins scored field goals on each of their first two possessions and led, 13–3, at halftime.

But I came back and so did the team. We only rushed for 56 yards, but I made a nice block on Monte Coleman, the Redskins linebacker, that sprung Joe Morris for a nine-yard touchdown that cut the score to 13–10. Then our defense made two big plays. Gary Reasons blocked a punt that Tom Flynn returned 27 yards for a touchdown. Then, on the next series, Pepper Johnson sacked Doug Williams and popped the ball loose. Jim Burt picked it up and ran 39 yards for another touchdown. It was his first in the NFL and he didn't climb a wall or anything like that, but I didn't care. We still won, 27–20.

Winning, and just playing again, felt good. It was good to go home that night, to Heidi and Brittany. I knew how proud Heidi was of me. We'd really done it, we'd really made it back.

Wednesday after the game, after we'd been watching films and getting ready for our next one against San Francisco, Bill came over to my locker.

"I can't believe how bad you played," he said. "You whiffed on Mann. You had 22 minus plays."

He just ripped me apart and told me I was worthless. And he said he was going to have to get another tackle in there.

More mind games.

I just told Bill that I'd been too hyped up. He knew that wasn't me. And he knew I'd settled down and played better later in the game. I just promised him that the next week would be different, that I'd be in control from the start, just the way he always wanted me to be.

And I was.

I played much better against San Francisco. It was a regular game, Sunday at one o'clock. There was no long wait, no long buildup. And I wasn't the focus anymore. I was just another offensive lineman, doing my job.

I settled down into a groove. I was stabbing people, and getting more confidence with every play. And I was playing a pretty good football game.

Joe Montana, the 49ers legend, didn't start that game. Steve Young, his high-priced backup, played the first half, and it was 10–10. Raul Allegre, our kicker, made a 36-yard field goal with nine seconds to go in the half to tie it. But I never saw it.

When we started that drive, we had a third-and-two on our own 37-yard line. For short yardage, Damian Johnson would move from right guard out to tight end and Doug Riesenberg would come in for Damian at guard.

It worked, with Joe Morris going over our blocks on the right side for a three-yard gain and the first down. But because of the NFL's rules on substitutions and eligible receivers, it meant that Damian had to go out for a play.

Doug stayed in at guard, and we were running a play-action pass. I got my guy, Jeff Stover, wired up right at the line. It turned out that that was the worst thing I could have done, because the rest of the line just collapsed.

Kevin Fagan sacked Phil Simms for a 13-yard loss on the play. Worse, Michael Carter, San Francisco's awesome nose tackle who had been an Olympic silver medalist in the shot put, just picked up Riesenberg and threw him like a rag doll. And Doug landed with his butt right on the outside of my leg, about five inches above the ankle.

I've seen the films of what happened next. Freeze-frame it and I'm standing there, straight up and blocking Stover, but my ankle and foot are flat on the ground at a 90-degree angle.

A white-heat pain shot through my ankle. I fell down, face first. And Joe Morris came over to me right away to see if I was all right.

I knew I was hurt. I got up and tried to put some weight on my foot, but I couldn't without pain exploding in my ankle.

Ronnie Barnes and Russ Warren helped me off the field. I couldn't even walk, couldn't put any pressure on my ankle at all. While I was over on the bench, with Russ checking it out, I heard Ronnie call up to the press box and give the standard Giants' line:

"Nelson, sprained ankle. Will return."

Will return? Whose ankle had he been looking at?

It was pretty close to halftime. Jumbo had gone in for me at right tackle and got called for holding on his first play. But Phil worked out of a second-and-33 with a big pass to Mark Ingram and an 11-yard run by Joe on fourth-and-two. Phil took us all the way to San Francisco's 19-yard line before the clock got him and we settled for Raul's field goal.

I saw some of that from the back of the cart while they ferried me into the locker room. When we got through the tunnel, I saw Bob McKittrick, the 49ers line coach, as he headed down from the press box to San Francisco's locker room. He stopped us for a minute, grabbed me and said, "I respect everything you've done. I just hope your ankle's all right."

Well, so did I.

They took me for X-rays and there was nothing broken, but Dr. Warren told me later it might have been better if something had been.

The ligaments holding the two bones in my lower leg together had stretched. Or torn. Russ told me the next day that as bad as it was, there was very little difference.

The bones had separated. They put me in a cold-compression boot for about an hour, then there was nothing else they could do. So I showered up and dressed and went back to the field on crutches.

Meanwhile, Heidi was up in her usual seat in the stands, frantic.

"I wanted to get up and run downstairs," she said, "but wives weren't allowed to do that. Some people behind me were listening to the game on radio, and they heard that Karl was going to be all right. I figured he would be. I knew that he had minor sprains every day. So I really thought he'd be back. I kept waiting, and he never came out. Then I saw him on crutches."

I got out there just in time to see us take the lead. The defense, again, had backed the 49ers up and Phil McConkey had returned a punt 32 yards to San Francisco's 15. Two plays later, Phil hit Lionel Manual for the touchdown that made it 17–13 with 1:21 to play.

But the defense had made one big mistake. They had knocked Young out of the game on a scramble at the end of the half. That meant Montana was in. And nobody is more dangerous at the end of a game than Joe Montana.

The 49ers got the ball on the kickoff and on 3rd-and-11 from his own 22, Montana looked deep for Jerry Rice.

Rice caught the ball and split between Kenny Hill and Mark Collins, who knocked each other off the tackle, and went all the way for a touchdown with 42 seconds to play.

I was just crushed. And though we didn't know it at the time, that touchdown was the difference between the 49ers making it to the playoffs with a 10–6 record and going on to win Super Bowl XXIII, and us sitting home with the same 10–6 record, not even qualified as a wild card.

I got home and I was just depressed, about the loss and about the injury.

"He had already done what I wanted him to do. He came back and played well, the way he had before. He played like the old Karl," Heidi said. "But this wasn't the way I wanted to see it end. To go through all that work and then have it end on a silly injury just killed me inside."

Chapter 10
The IR Zone

I was invisible. I was back in the zone.

The day after the San Francisco game, I was walking down the hall to the meeting room to look at the films. Parcells came out of the coach's locker room and started walking towards me. Suddenly he found something really interesting on the wall opposite where I was.

He couldn't even look at me. He couldn't say a word, couldn't say anything to me.

Originally, I was supposed to be out from two to four weeks. Then it was four to six. I stayed active for one more game, and every day Bill would ask, "So, you ready to practice?" But I was still on crutches. They ended up putting me on IR.

Bill was just being hopeful. After all, I'd done a year's worth of shoulder rehab in just seven months. Maybe he thought I'd come back quicker from this, too, and he was trying to push me to see if I could do it. But Russ knew from the start that I couldn't.

I think it just gave Bill something to talk about. He was just busting my chops. Most days, he would tell me how good Riesenberg was playing, as if that was going to get me back faster.

The players treated me pretty much the same way, putting me in the zone. Even when I was playing again, not everybody knew what to say or do. I was still a little bit like a freak show. Most of the guys on the offensive line, the ones who knew me best, accepted me back. But a lot of them were thinking, What's this guy doing back playing football again? Why is he bothering?

But nobody asked me about it, not once.

They were just afraid of the cancer. And when I hurt my ankle, it made it easier for people not to deal with me. I was put on the shelf by everybody. I'd be standing talking to somebody and a coach would walk by, and people got real uncomfortable. When you're a player, you don't want to be seen talking to somebody on IR.

There were some exceptions, though. Harry Carson helped me out a lot. I'd be sitting in the trainer's room, and Bill would come in to see the three or four other guys who were hurt. He'd ask each one, "How you doin'?"

And he'd ignore me. But Harry would always say, real loud, "Well, Karl, how you doin' today?"

I'd say, real loud, "Fine, Harry. My ankle's doing pretty good, but I'm not ready to practice yet. And thanks for asking."

Bill would just walk out. He'd always say something to the other guys, something about me. He felt obligated, I guess, because Harry had embarrassed him.

But players took their cues from Bill. They didn't want to be around a guy on IR. I don't know whether it's because you never know when you're going to be the next guy to go down and you don't want to think about it, and seeing one of us hurt makes you think about it. Or maybe you just don't want to be associated with someone who's hurt. Bill was paranoid about guys who were hurt a lot. And if he saw you standing next to somebody on IR, he's going to associate the two of you. You didn't want that to happen.

It was just a really weird situation.

Bill had a tough time handling my having cancer. But when it came to an ankle injury, he knew just how to treat me, and that was like dirt.

He tried to avoid me, but he couldn't. And I think he was really pulling for me. He wanted me to get back and play well. He was very upset when I didn't play well against Washington and he let me know it. I don't know—maybe he had his mind made up that I wasn't going to be the player that I was before, because I wasn't. That was because of the shoulder. It wasn't because of the cancer.

I don't think he was relieved when I got hurt. I don't think he was ready to bench me, because there were a lot of problems with the offensive line against San Francisco before I got hurt. And even if I wasn't going to be as good as I had been, I thought that half of Karl Nelson was better than a lot of those guys.

I knew that Jumbo wasn't ready to go. He became a good player for the Giants, helping them win Super Bowl XXV, but he had a long way to go. And Doug wasn't the answer yet. So Bill couldn't have been relieved. He still needed me.

I had started to play better against San Francisco and I was still a pretty good tackle. I just never got into the swing of things that year. But I think as time went on, I would have.

On IR, my routine was to go down to Giants Stadium at 8:30 a.m. and get treatment for an hour. Then I'd wait for the meetings at 10. I'd go to practice and ride the stationary bikes as much as I could. I tried to run, going at a slow jog, but it hurt like hell. I asked Russ about it and he said I was better off doing nothing.

"Don't push it right now," he said. "You've got to let the ligaments that hold the two bones together heal up. Every time you run on it, you're just pushing those bones further apart."

So I stayed off it. Then after practice, I'd get more treatment from Mike Ryan. Ice, electrostimulation, sound treatments, whatever.

I was extremely frustrated. I could handle not playing the year before because I had cancer. But I always had said that an ankle injury is something you tape up and you play on. I had never had an ankle I couldn't play on before. I had had them swell up like crazy, but I'd just put enough tape on to be able to play.

Only this wasn't a true ankle injury. It was a sprain where the bones join the ankle, a sprain of the ligaments holding those bones together. When a player sprains an ankle by rolling it to the outside, that's just a stabilization injury. He gets an orthoplast stirrup and tapes it to the ankle so there's no way the ankle can bend. Then he plays.

This time, I couldn't bear any weight on my ankle, so I couldn't even practice, let alone play. And sitting home, watching games on TV, drove me nuts.

But that's the way I had to do it. Bill wouldn't let me watch from the sidelines. He wouldn't let any IR guys on the sidelines. At the end of the season, he forced Harry onto IR, but Harry still came to the games and made it down to the sidelines. That upset me a little, but I knew Harry was an exceptional case. He probably just walked past the security guards, knowing they wouldn't stop him.

I didn't do that. And Bill didn't want me there. He said he'd get me two tickets in the stands. I offered to do the games on radio, but WNEW said it was a conflict since, technically, I was still on the roster. So I just stayed home and watched the games on TV.

Bill finally started talking to me on October 6, talking to me as a football player again. The night before, I'd seen Dr. Warren after practice. He said my ankle was looking good, even though I still had a lot of pain and some tender spots. But it was something I could work through.

Bill knew I'd gotten the thumbs-up. So he started talking about getting ready to practice. He was starting to include me in his thought patterns.

Russ told me to start practicing the next Wednesday, October 12. But that day, my first day back, nobody even told Fred Hoaglin, my line coach, that I was going to be ready.

So I got absolutely zero reps with the first team. And I thought, I'm back practicing, let's get me in the swing.

But Bill wasn't going to activate me.

My thought was that if I could practice, I could play. And after practice I asked Bill about it.

He said, "It's only your first day."

It was driving me nuts. I figured I'd get my job back as soon as I was ready. That's the old coach's line, that a starter doesn't lose his job because of an injury. Of course, they only use that when they want the starter to come back and play.

But I had to sit home and watch another game on TV. The Giants beat Detroit 30–10 to go 4–3. I'd practiced all week and I was still sitting at home. It made it much, much tougher. One stupid play that wasn't even my fault. Riesenberg fell on my ankle, and there I was watching on TV, after all I'd been through. I had cancer and came back and played, and I was out because of a stupid ankle injury.

The next week in practice, I started working with George Martin to get my timing down. You really don't get enough reps in practice, so I asked George to help me afterward. I just wanted to show Bill I was serious about wanting to play.

I felt I was better than Doug, but he was still starting, and I was on IR. And Bill was still questioning how tough I was. He only mentioned it two or three hundred times a day, asking if I could still take the pressure.

It bothered me, but I didn't question him. He was the coach, right? And I never went through a third party, somebody like George Martin, either. I wouldn't do that.

I just waited.

Finally, Damian Johnson's back started bothering him. He'd been hurt against Philadelphia on October 10, and they were debating about putting him on IR.

Bill came up and said, "I've got a lot of options."

He was wondering if he should keep Doug at right tackle and make Joe Fields, our veteran backup center who'd come over from the Jets, responsible for handling right guard. Or should he use Mike Ariey or Gary Schippang?

"Or," he said, "Do I activate you to back up at guard and tackle?"

He was really messing with my head, telling me all his options when I knew he really wanted to activate me. At least that's what I was hoping. And that's what he did, pulling me off IR on October 22. Even though I heard about it from two or three people, I didn't hear it officially from Bill.

That was a Saturday, and the Giants were playing down in Atlanta the next day. I didn't get in for a single play. It was the first game, since forever, that I hadn't played in a game I was eligible to play in. The first one in any sport in my life.

I called it an "ERW." Eat, ride, warm-up.

It was sickening to watch the whole game from the sidelines and not be in there. I stood by Fred the whole time and listened to the play calls as they went in. I watched the game, and as the guys came off the field I'd talk to them. It was hard, because I felt I should be in there, but I was still a team guy trying to help any way I could. Mostly, I'd talk to Doug about right tackle.

After the game, I sat there wondering how I could play next year if I couldn't get in now?

I started thinking there wasn't going to be a spot for me on this team. I was ready to use the NFL's Plan B system to find a team that would take me. But if I wasn't playing here, who else was going to want me?

When I got home, Heidi and I talked it over. And it got more serious later that week.

That Wednesday, the first real practice day of the week, I was finally starting to get some work with the first team. I was in for five plays in the nine-on-seven drill when John Washington, one of our defensive lineman, fell on my ankle, the same way Riesenberg had in the San Francisco game. I just lay there in pain, screaming.

It hurt so much I could barely walk, but I knew I had to get back to practice or Bill was going to put me back on IR. So I came back and hopped around on one leg.

When practice was ending, I went up to him and said, "Bill, my ankle's pretty messed up. Let me ride the bike instead of the sprints."

And he said, "If you can't run, you can't play."

So I ran the sprints on one leg.

In the locker room after practice I was at my cubicle which kind of sits in the middle of the room, facing a long row of lockers. Bill walked by and, suddenly, he fell down and grabbed his ankle and started yelling, "Oh! My ankle! My ankle!"

He thought he was really funny, but I was so mad. I don't think I said anything to him, but I should have. I would now, but I wouldn't back then.

He was still the coach. And I had a problem talking to people in authority. So it was tough to talk back to him, or say what was on my mind.

That night, my throbbing ankle had me up all night. Heidi was very upset about it and upset that I wasn't playing. It was causing a lot of tension for us.

We were worried about what would happen the next year. I had a bad ankle and a bad shoulder and arthritis in my knee that's kept me from doing squats for three years. I knew that if I went out on Plan B, I probably wasn't going to start anywhere, but possibly I could have been a backup. And that would have been all right. Because, as Heidi pointed out, every year I'd been a starter with the Giants, my backups—William Roberts, Conrad Goode, Gordon King, Jumbo Elliot—had made more money than I had. Substantially more.

I was ready to go anywhere to get a job, because I knew I wasn't going to have one with the Giants. Bill said he had plans for me for the next year, but I didn't know if I could believe him.

"Bill is becoming your worst nightmare," Heidi said. "You're coming home every day, with no spirit in you. You're like a hurt puppy dog. Your guts have been ripped out, and I have to deal with it. So maybe it's time we went somewhere else and settled for less money. You can sit on the bench and not get banged up."

We had just bought our house and the plan had been to pay it off before I retired. That meant another two or three years. The problem was, I'd have to find a team that wouldn't force me to do squats and other lifts—things that I couldn't do because of the wear and tear on my body.

My ankle would eventually heal, but my shoulder and knee

were going to be problems. I figured that a guy who'd played as many NFL games as I had, though, and been as successful, could get a shot somewhere, even if it was as a backup.

So we were thinking of going somewhere else. The comeback had turned into a comedown. I thought I'd make it back, make the Pro Bowl and then play another year or two to go out in style. But that dream was crushed when Bill didn't bring me off IR as soon as he could have. And it was buried, dug deeply into the ground, when I was activated, but wasn't given a chance to play.

It was tough. I spoke to Bill when he was going through his heart problems in 1992. He had two angioplasties and then open-heart surgery. And he told me, "I knew you had all those surgeries done for the cancer. And I thought if Karl can do it, I can handle it."

It made me feel really good that he was thinking about me and the things I went through and that that gave him some strength.

But in '88, the relationship was hard. I didn't mind when he was busting my chops. In preseason, he used to tell me, "I'm sick and tired of answering Karl Nelson questions. That's all I do. You're getting all this sympathy, all this good will. Thank God the football season's here and I can quit answering them."

He was joking around, absolutely. He was very happy I was coming back. When Bill starts joking around with you, you know everything's cool.

But he wasn't joking the day after John Washington fell on my ankle. He passed the word down through Barnes: "No practice today, you're back on IR."

My ankle hurt like hell and I could barely move it, but I had to practice. If I went back on IR, that would be it for the season.

I practiced. My reward? Bill started calling me "Mr. Charlton Heston" for my "acting" ability.

We played Detroit and I got another ERW, but a week later, November 6, I got to play against Dallas. Doug got hurt, and he put Jumbo in ahead of me, which really ticked me off. It was Bill's call.

It wasn't a big surprise. Jumbo had been running ahead of me in practice. But it still hurt pretty bad when I heard him yell, "Jumbo, get in there."

I didn't throw my helmet or anything. I stayed under control, just waiting next to Fred. And Jumbo gave up a sack in the first five or six plays, so I went in for him. I played six plays and then the game was over.

But we'd won, our fourth in a row, and we were 7–3. And I'd played. So I was pretty happy when I got home.

And the first thing I heard when I walked in the door was Heidi, saying, "We've got a problem here."

My parents had come in for that weekend and they had been home with Heidi watching the game. I could have gotten them tickets, but my dad doesn't like going to the stadium unless I'm going to be playing. And it didn't look like I was going to be playing. So they stayed home.

During the game, Doug was having some problems. On TV, you could see me standing next to Parcells on the sidelines and my dad kept saying, "They're going to pull Reisenberg and put Karl in." I hadn't told him that Jumbo was running ahead of me in practice as Doug's backup.

Heidi, who knew what was going on between Bill and me, said, "No, they're not."

"If they don't," my dad said, "it's because of reasons like that, you talking him into the fact that he's never going to play again."

He was frustrated because he wanted to see me play and he blamed Heidi for the problems I was having. But we never told my family about the problems I was having with Bill. As far as they were concerned, we still had a great relationship. My father thought Bill was going to put me in because he thought I was one of Bill's "guys." Heidi knew the real story.

It was the same with the cancer. I didn't really tell my parents what was going on. Heidi had to do that. But when she did, they didn't believe her because they didn't want to believe her.

I should have been honest with them, kept them informed. My lack of communication with them had caused a lot of conflicts. This time, Heidi exploded.

She told my father to pack his bags and get out of our house. Then she stormed up to our bedroom.

She was thinking, How am I going to handle this? My husband's whole life has been stomped on to the point where he's got no heart left, nothing to make him feel good. Now that he's finally gotten into a game and he's going to come home on top of the world, I'm going to tear him apart because I've told his father to get out of our house.

At age one, they handed me a ball and told me to smile. It was the wrong-shaped ball, but I'm already working on my game face. *Inset:* That's me in the middle, with my sister Karen and brother Kevin.
Credit: Nelson collection

The DeKalb South Middle School basketball team. I'm the fourth guy on one knee from the left. Notice how they're keeping the ball away from me. They knew I'd be an offensive lineman. *Credit: Nelson collection*

Posing for the photographer in 1974, my freshman year in high school. *Inset:* DeKalb High School, Class of '78. *Credit: Nelson collection*

The Nelson family portrait, circa
1975. From left to right: Mom, sister
Karen, brother Kevin, me, Dad.
Inset: Earlier days
Credit: Nelson collection

My senior year at Iowa State
University. I believe it was the last
time they let me touch the ball.
Credit: Nelson collection

Our wedding day—April 27, 1985. Now you know why they say Heidi is my "better half."
Credit: Nelson collection

As a Giant, getting mentally prepared for the next offensive series. This is Heidi's favorite photo of me. *Credit: Dave Austin*

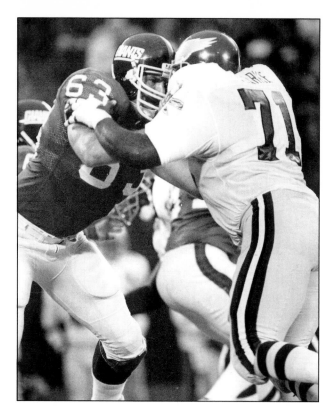

Life on the line in the NFL.
A play action pass against the
Philadelphia Eagles.
Credit: Jerry Pinkus

A draw play from the
1986 Super Bowl season.
Credit: Jerry Pinkus

Joe Morris and me executing the "slant counter special" in Super Bowl XXI. This play went for some big yardage. *Inset:* Five of the happiest and most confident Giants fans, even before our Super Bowl XXI victory over the Denver Broncos. From left to right: Heidi, Linda Morris, Diana Simms, Michelle Oates, and Linda Taylor.
Credit: Jerry Pinkus

During our 1987 visit to the White House, President Reagan honored us as Super Bowl champions. That's me, Senator Nelson, all the way in the back. That's the price you pay for being tall.
Credit: Jerry Pinkus

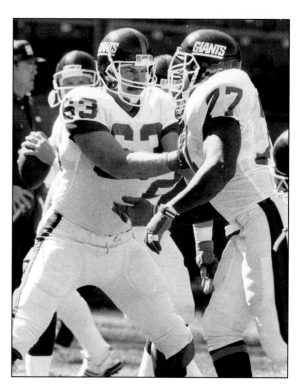

Pre-game warm-ups during the 1987 season with Eric Dorsey (77). I can tell by looking at this picture that my left shoulder is bothering me.
Credit: Jerry Pinkus

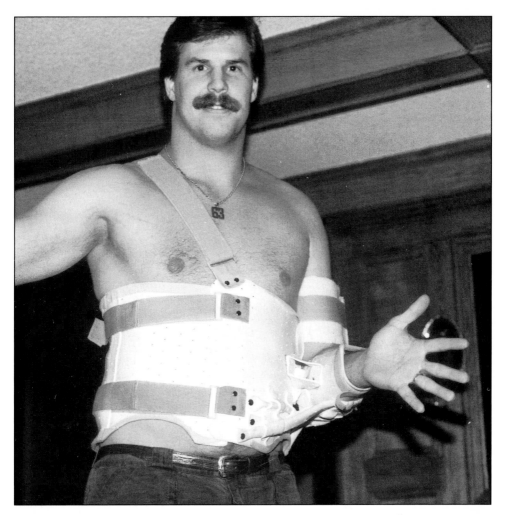

So much for a simple 'scope of my shoulder. After this major shoulder surgery, I was in this brace for six weeks. *Credit: Nelson collection*

Brittany and Heidi visiting me in the hospital after my operation. Heidi was smiling, although she didn't know if this would be one of the last family photos she would have with me.
Credit: Nelson collection

A Nelson family portrait, while I was undergoing chemotherapy treatments. Yes, that is me on the left with no hair but, more importantly, no mustache.
Credit: Nelson collection

Fighting to live, with my newborn daughter Lyndsay on my lap. If a picture's worth a thousand words, well...
Credit: Nelson collection

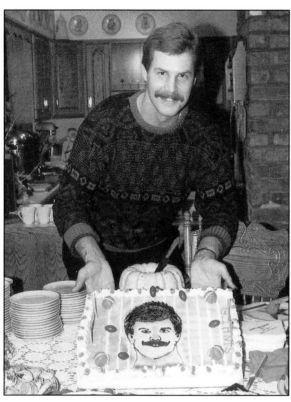

About to serve myself at my surprise party. The hair and mustache did come back!
Credit: Nelson collection

One of the many charity events I enjoy going to, the SportsChannel/Leukemia Society of America's New York Athlete of the Year Award Dinner. This photo is special because it is with teammate Phil Simms; my support system and fellow Hodgkin's survivor, Olympic Gold Medalist Jeff Blatnick; and class act John Amos, who has personally helped Heidi and me with some of our charity events.
Credit: Nelson collection

Getting ready for the "Tailgate Show" radio broadcast in the parking lot of Giants Stadium with the greatest fans in the world. *Inset:* One of the many special guests we have during the "Tailgate Show." Bet you didn't know that was Jon Bon Jovi all the way to the right! Our engineer, Tom Tracy, is on my right with my co-host, Bob Papa, between Jon and me. *Credit: Jerry Pinkus*

Lyndsay and Brittany doing their jockey imitation, with me as Secretariat. Gitty-up, Daddy—go faster! *Credit: Nelson collection*

Receiving the Tomorrows Children's Fund "Sportsman of the Year" Award from my good friend and former teammate George Martin. *Credit: Jerry Pinkus*

Brittany, Heidi, and Lyndsay in front of me, Christmas 1990. Here's to good health. Boy, did we have something to celebrate! *Credit: Nelson collection*

That's me with Brittany, and Heidi with Lyndsay. They say Brittany takes after me, but looks like Heidi. And Lyndsay takes after Heidi, but looks like me. What do you think?
Credit: Nelson collection

The girls and me in Florida with my grandparents, Paul and Alta Elliott, 1992.
Credit: Nelson collection

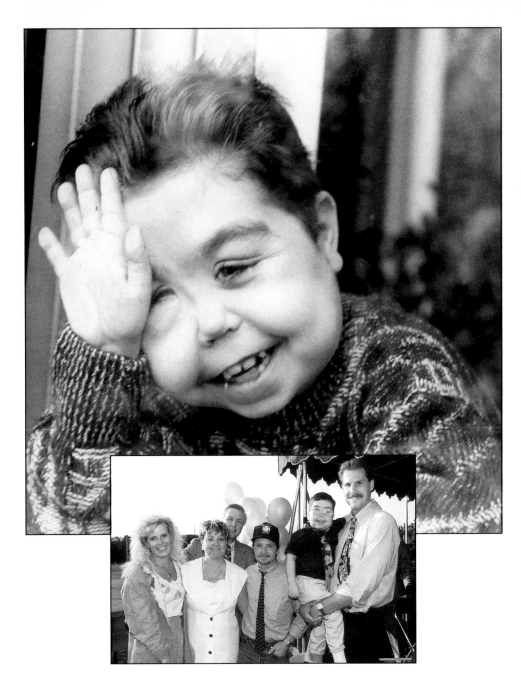

Michael Gillick, the most remarkable fourteen-year-old boy I've ever met. He's been a great inspiration to me. *Inset:* From left to right: Heidi, Linda and Rusty Gillick (Michael's parents), Michael J. Fox, Michael, and me at an Ocean of Love fund-raiser. *Credit: Nelson collection*

So she went downstairs. She told my mother, "I'm sorry, but it's not my fault he's not starting. I'm the one who's here, to pick up the pieces every day. I don't need this thrown at me."

Then my father walked in and they talked. Before I got home, it was patched up to the point where they were civil to each other. Then I got home and she told me about it.

It wasn't easy on any of us.

After playing against Dallas, I ERW'd the next weekend at Phoenix, so I went to Bill and asked him what the deal was.

"Don't get paranoid," he told me.

Don't get paranoid? He told Godfrey the same thing, and then cut him. Just because they call you paranoid doesn't mean they're not out to get you.

Maybe I was paranoid. I certainly had a hard time dealing with what was going on. The night after the Phoenix game, Heidi and I went to a dinner at the Loews Glenpointe Hotel where I got an award as the New Jersey Special Olympics Professional Athlete of the Year.

I did the dinner because of Joe Morris. Special Olympics was Joe's charity, and he was their celebrity chairperson. Back then, all the players would help each other out. One guy would do a charity and everybody would show up whenever that guy asked them to.

But this one was hard for me. I didn't know what to say.

I got up and said, "I feel pretty funny about getting this award, considering I've only played a game and a half in the last two years. But playing football gives me the opportunity to help people.

"You need someone to open up your eyes to the big picture and Heidi did that for me. She showed me that I had to get myself better first and stop worrying about football. And that gave me an opportunity to open a lot of people's eyes. Once you've been told you've got cancer, that doesn't mean you're going to die. You have the ability to get treatments and go on with your life."

Even though I wasn't playing, I tried to turn that into a positive. I thought the speech was extremely well received.

About that time, Harry Carson got his knee 'scoped. That's when I became Harry's buddy, to pay him back.

"Hey, Harry, buddy. I'll talk to you, even though you're hurt!"

A lot of other guys thought I was nuts. Bill had put him on IR, against Harry's very public protests. It was Harry's last season, but Bill wanted to have a full complement of bodies and Harry was going to be out for up to four weeks. So he put Harry on IR and the rest of the players stopped talking to one of the most respected guys on our team and in the NFL. Harry had moved into the zone.

Meanwhile, I could see Bill moving Elliot and Moore ahead of me. He was thinking about a youth movement. But when Doug got banged up against Philadelphia on November 20, I went in ahead of Jumbo. That made me feel pretty good.

The next week, I spent most of the practice time with the first team. Bill still wouldn't tell me if I was playing or not, but I had a feeling. Friday morning, he still hadn't told me. Finally, Fred Hoaglin told me Saturday morning in our hotel in New Orleans. Bill didn't mention it until Sunday.

That was the game where Phil Simms was hurt and Jeff Hostetler played the first half. Jeff was yanked for Jeff Rutledge in the second half. We all thought Hoss was hurt. I didn't know until way after the game when I asked him if he was okay, and he said, "Yeah, why?"

"They say you got hurt."

"No, they benched me."

He was very upset about that, and still is. But honestly, we wouldn't have won the game if he had stayed in, not at that point in his career. It was close and we weren't scoring a lot of points, but we came back and won 13–12 on Lawrence Taylor's heroics in what was probably the best game of his Hall of Fame career.

I played the whole game against Frank Warren, a big moose. Our first offensive play was a run, and when I hit him it felt like a brick wall. I didn't have the same drive because of my ankle and shoulder. It was an absolute war for me, which was great because I needed that to get going again. I blocked Warren and Rickey Jackson, the Saints' linebacker, quite a bit, and I didn't give up a sack.

I thought I'd play again the next week, but they made a game-time decision on Riesenberg's health and he went all the way against Phoenix. I got in on short-yardage plays. This time, I'd be at right tackle and Doug would go to tight end. Then he had to sit out a play, so I'd get the next one, too.

At least I was playing on some kind of regular basis. But that's when Bill decided I wasn't allowed in the trainer's room anymore.

I had been icing down every day after practice: Knee, ankle, shoulder. But Bill said I was just thinking I was hurt when I wasn't really hurt. And because I wasn't hurt, according to his thinking, I didn't need to be in the trainer's room.

I had Ronnie Barnes fill up a cooler with ice and bring it out to my locker, since I couldn't go in and get it. And I did that for a few days until Bill wouldn't allow that either. Then I had to stop at a deli on my way home from practice every day, just to buy my ice.

Bill was just being totally unreasonable. If you can take care of your body and get more out of it by icing it, then why not ice it? It's what I'd been doing my entire career.

Of course, most football players would never allow the coach to see them being iced because it bothers the coaches. But I knew that ice would make me feel better and I'd be able to play longer. Ice keeps down the inflammation in the joints, and if you play football, you've got inflammation.

After every game a pitcher pitches, he throws his elbow and shoulder into ice. Why not take care of your body? What's wrong with that?

Well, there must be something, because Bill wouldn't let me do it. And Ronnie wouldn't stand up to him, either.

I never complained. I just told Harry, "I can't come see you anymore."

I still haven't figured out why Bill did it. I guess he just didn't like seeing me in there. He diagnosed me as a hypochondriac.

Bill has his own explanation:

"Ronnie Barnes told me he was afraid Nelson was developing what we called a 'hospital mentality.' He was used to going in, receiving his treatments.

"I said, 'Is it detrimental if he doesn't get them?'

"And he said, 'No, we've just got to get him out of that mentality.'

"Now, some guys develop habits. There are places they're comfortable, things they're comfortable doing. But the trainer's room is a bad place to be comfortable for a pro athlete. Take Mark Bavaro. He had some very serious problems, but he never enjoyed going in there. He wanted to get in and get out as quick as he could. Some guys like to hang out in there. So to try to get Karl out of that habit, I just wouldn't let him in."

Deep down, Bill knew that he was treating me differently as an injured player than he had as a cancer patient.

"You don't ignore the injuries," Bill said. "But it's just one of a myriad of things in the sport. So, yes, you treat them differently than a kid with a disease, or one with a spinal injury or something more threatening. I don't want to say you get callous, but you don't react."

But I just wanted to take care of my body and there shouldn't be anything wrong with that. I've always done what it takes to be ready to play. I never missed a workout, never missed a practice, never missed a game, unless I was really hurt. And he should have known that.

I put up with it because the season was almost over. We played our last game December 18 against the Jets. If we won, we'd be the NFC Eastern Division champs.

We were trailing 20–14 the first time we got the ball in the fourth quarter. Phil took us on an 80-yard drive. We had three short-yardage situations on the way, so I was in on six of the 11 plays, including Phil's nine-yard touchdown pass to Lionel Manuel that put us up 21–20 with 4:54 to play.

The Jets came back to beat us on Ken O'Brien's pass to Al Toon with 37 seconds left. And that, along with the 49ers' loss to the Los Angeles Rams the next night, knocked us out of the playoffs.

So it didn't end on a high note. But I'll always be able to say we scored a touchdown on the last play I ever played.

Chapter 11
Round 2

There was one play in that game against the Jets, in the third quarter, when Doug Riesenberg hurt his ankle.

He was sitting there on the turf, taking a while to get up. And Parcells yelled, "Nelson, get in there!"

I took two steps onto the field and thought, I don't really want to go.

That had never happened before.

Doug got up, and I saw he was going to be all right. But I guess I already knew the cancer was back. I was tired and run down, and there was this lump in my neck. And I thought, This game's not that important to me anymore.

I was glad to go in on short-yardage plays and stay in the next play. That was fine. But after everything that had happened that frustrating season, I didn't want to go in as Doug's backup. It was weird and I can't explain it or understand it. I just didn't think I should be in there. I don't know whether it was because I was sick or because of all the bull that Parcells had put me through.

Whatever it was, I hesitated. Bill wanted me in, but I stopped and came back to the sideline when I saw Doug getting up. The trainers never went out, so Doug didn't have to miss a play.

There was a lot of weird stuff going through my head right then. For some reason, I didn't want to go in. Then the moment passed.

I'd never admitted to myself that I was sick until then.

The week before we played New Orleans, the last week of November, I started having a lot of extra muscle soreness, more than I should have been having because I really wasn't practicing that much. It was all-over soreness. It didn't ring a bell in my head, but that was the start of the cancer coming back.

I was sore and tired. After the game, it was worse, but I thought it was because it had been a long time since I had played that hard, with such high-speed contact, for 45 plays.

A couple of weeks later, on December 7, I was really drained after practice. I thought I was having a problem with my thyroid.

About the time I'd gone on IR, I'd had a routine checkup from Dr. Wolf and he found that my thyroid gland had shut down because of the radiation. Maybe that's why I hadn't been real sharp against Washington and San Francisco. But it wasn't a big problem. He put me on a medication that regulates the metabolism in place of the thyroid.

I was so tired, I thought I needed the dosage adjusted. But I had another checkup with Dr. Wolf scheduled for the next week, so I didn't worry.

I hadn't even told Heidi about being tired and sore. She was eight months' pregnant and I didn't want to worry her. I thought it was the thyroid, all the way.

On December 13, the Tuesday before the Jets game, I went to see Dr. Wolf.

"I'm tired," I told him. "I think you ought to check the medication."

"As long as you're here," he said, "let's do a full exam."

He started feeling and poking around my neck.

"How have you been feeling?" he asked.

"I have a cold," I said, "but I always have a cold during the football season."

"Well, there's a lump here. I want to check it out, and take some extra blood tests to see if it's an infection. Or it may be just a swollen gland."

Then he told me that if it was anything, it was at a very, very early stage.

That night, I couldn't sleep. That's the first time that "cancer" clicked in.

Over the next few days, the left side of my neck became sore, but I think that was more psychosomatic. Dr. Wolf had told Dr. Warren about the lump he'd found. At practice Thursday, Russ came over to me and told me he wanted to take a look at my shoulder, but all the time he was really feeling for the lump. I didn't realize that until later.

All this was in my mind while we played the Jets. Two days after the game, I went to see Dr. Wolf, and he told me he wanted to take the lump out, as quickly as he could.

That was December 20, the night of our Christmas party when I called Heidi to tell her I'd be late and showed up with the bucket of Roy Rogers' fried chicken and the very bad news.

Somehow, we made it through that party and when it was over, we found ourselves lying in bed. And we both knew.

At the party, some people were really bummed out about the Giants. But if we'd won and made the playoffs, it would have been a real zoo. Ronnie Barnes told me, "We don't fool around with things like that. You'd have been put on IR and that was it. We'd get this taken care of."

Can you imagine what it would have been like during the playoffs, even if we'd had the week off with a division title?

It was crazy enough as it was.

And it was already the worst Christmas you can imagine.

I had the lump taken out by Dr. John Whitsel II, one of Wolf's associates at New York Hospital. They did it under local anesthesia, so I was awake for the whole procedure.

To start, the operating table was very narrow, and very short. They had to put an extension on it so my feet wouldn't hang off. Then they laid me down, with my arms spread out and an IV line in each one to put in the liquids and a heavy dose of tranquilizers.

While I was sitting up, Dr. Whitsel felt for the lump and located it. But when I was lying down, he lost it. So I had to sit up again, with my arms perfectly straight. There was a person on each side holding my arms up.

Dr. Whitsel found the lump again and this time he kept his fingers on it while I lay back.

"Oh, there it is! It's behind your collarbone. Now I know where I have to go."

They decided it would be easier for them if they elevated my head. But they'd positioned me on the table wrongly and my head was where my feet should have been. And that end of the table only went up 10 degrees, instead of the 30 degree angle they wanted. But I'll tell you, with the stuff they were pumping into me, I didn't care where I was.

The low angle made the procedure take longer than it should have. What was supposed to be a 20-minute procedure took 45 minutes. Dr. Whitsel had to dig under the collarbone. He got the lump out in one big piece, but the cancer had already spread. Sometimes, you do a cancer surgery and that's all you have to do. But Hodgkin's is a disease of the lymph system. Even though it appears to be in one location, cancer cells may have moved to nearby lymph nodes. Surgery isn't guaranteed to get it all.

I went home that night, with Heidi and Jay Ferreira, one of our closest friends. They had driven me into the city and had gone to Rusty's for lunch while I had the surgery.

As soon as it was done, the doctors looked at the lump and knew it was Hodgkin's again. There was very little question in their minds, and none in ours. This time, it was called "atypical" Hodgkin's. Dr. Wolf explained that meant that since the area had been altered by the radiation, it was masked so it could have looked like other things. Since I'd already had Hodgkin's, they knew that it was a recurrence, but an atypical recurrence.

There were a few more tests. I had a gallium scan and another MRI. And then we went to see Dr. Wolf.

"How long do you want to keep playing football?" he asked.

"I'd like to play another year or two," I told him. "Why?"

"Well, that might make a difference in how I'm going to treat you."

I stopped him short.

"No, it doesn't," I said. "You do whatever you have to do. Football's not important to me anymore."

(Heidi had gotten my head straightened out.)

Dr. Wolf told me, "If I'm going to treat you full bore, you probably won't be able to play again."

I said, "I don't care. Football's not important right now. Getting healthy is all that's important right now."

The first time, football's what got me through. The second time, it was my family and making sure I was going to be here for them. Football wasn't important at all. I pretty much knew I wasn't going to play again. Even before the cancer came back, I knew I'd have a tough time making any club. I wasn't even sure I could pass a physical with my shoulder problems.

Then Dr. Wolf said, "We're going to hit you pretty hard. I'm going to give you large doses."

Chemotherapy is given according to your surface area, and they determine that from your height and weight. Dr. Wolf had never treated anybody with my surface area before. I think he was giving me more chemo than he'd ever given anybody else he'd treated.

I tried to be ready for it. When he first told me he wanted to take the lump out, I'd asked him if it was Hodgkin's again, how he was going to treat it.

So I knew it was chemo. The first time through, with

radiation, I knew absolutely nothing. I never knew anybody who had cancer, other than through Tomorrow's Children. When the doctors told me I'd get radiation, I wasn't afraid, because the next thing they said was that I had a 90 percent chance of a cure.

The first time, I didn't know enough to be scared. The second time, I knew. I knew they could treat it and they were doing a lot of new things. But I also knew what cancer was and that it could kill me. And I knew that the odds had dropped from 90 percent—lucky me, to be in the 10 percent—to 75 percent.

I'd been told they were going to get it the first time, and they didn't. Then it came back, and now they were telling me they were going to get it, but the odds were lower. Now, I didn't know what to think.

I learned it isn't a numbers game. If you want to play the odds, go to Atlantic City. With cancer, you forget about the numbers and you deal with it.

Dr. Wolf explained that the combination of radiation and the chemo he was going to give me increased the chances I'd get leukemia. That's something I'm still living with. I didn't ask the odds on that. I don't want to know. The numbers aren't really that important. I had to cure the cancer first. If I ever get that type of leukemia, I'll have to hope there's a cure for that. Right now, there isn't one.

There's no real choice. People always say I was so brave and courageous to go through the cancer treatments. Well, what was my option?

There are two ways to approach it: You can give up, which I guess is not the brave thing to do. Or you can be positive. People would say, "I don't know how you handled it." Well, you find a way.

Would this be high on my list of things to do again? No. But if they say this is your situation and you can stick your head in the sand and die, or you can find a way to get treatments and make it through, I don't think that's a hard choice. You just do what you have to do to survive.

But I do know a lot of people go the other way. I have people who wrote telling me, "I had a family member who was diagnosed with cancer and wasn't going to get treatments, but because they heard your story, they're going to."

Generally when someone gets cancer, they go through three phases. There's denial, then depression, and, finally, the get-on-with-it phase. The first time, I completely skipped over the first two. The first thing I wanted to know (and the only thing I wanted to know) was what I had to do to get better, to get well enough to play football again.

The second time, I had a day of denial, a day of depression, and then moved on. I did say, "I hope it's not cancer because I know more about chemo and I don't know if I can take it." That's denial, and maybe a little bit of depression. I went through it the night of our Christmas party, lying in bed with Heidi. And it was just between us. We came to terms with the fact that it was back. By the time Dr. Wolf told us I had Hodgkin's again, I was already prepared. I'd been through denial and depression, or as much of it as I was going to go through. I was ready to move on.

That's what it's all about. If you stay in denial too long, it may be too late.

Parcells always said, "The only way to get through something you don't like is to bitch about it." That's perfect for training camp. Nobody likes training camp. But to get through it, you bitch and you moan and you cry. And in five-and-a-half weeks it's over and you get to play some real football.

With this, though, I tried not to complain at all or to ask, why me?

I probably should have complained a little more. When I talked to the press, I tried to stay very positive. It wasn't an act, it's just the type of person I am.

But other people with cancer had their friends saying, "You have the same thing Karl Nelson has. How come you're not handling it as well?"

That really bothered me when I heard about it. Truth is, there were days I didn't handle it well. But I always wanted to put forth a positive image. If I had to do it again, I would stress that I had a lot of bad days. I just tried to get through them.

It started with Dr. Wolf. He said, "We're going to hammer you with chemo." And then he went through the potential side effects, which is a long, long list.

That's when I knew it was true what cancer patients say: Most people don't die from cancer, they die from treatment.

There are certain drugs used that are extremely toxic to your heart, other ones that are very toxic to the lungs. Essentially, chemotherapy attacks the fast-reproducing cells in your body. Cancer cells reproduce about 100 times faster than normal cells. That's why you lose your hair, skin, sperm, mucus, saliva, and nails. Anything that reproduces quickly is going to be attacked. That's what chemotherapy is designed to do—find those cells and hammer 'em.

Dr. Wolf laid it all out. Then he called experts all over the country because of my size, and sent slides of the lump tissue to them.

At this point, we hadn't said anything to the press. It was such a circus the first time, and Heidi was far along in her pregnancy. We didn't want it to get out until we were ready, and we weren't ready.

That was tricky. Like January 3, the day I got my bone marrow test. I finished the test and was having lunch in a diner in New York. A guy came up to me. He must have been about 25, and he said, "I have Hodgkin's and you've been a big inspiration to me. I know you beat it, and you're doing great, and that makes me feel good." It made me feel like crap. I couldn't tell him the Hodgkin's was back. We just didn't want to tell anybody.

Our game plan was to get a new phone line at the house, with a number we'd only give our family and close friends. We'd hook the old number to an answering machine. Then we'd have a press conference. The Giants were great. They said, "Just let us know how you want to do it, and we'll set it up."

I still had to have a lot of tests done. I had an MRI, feet first again. See, I knew the drill. I had plenty of other new tests, too. An echocardiogram for my heart, and a lung test. They want "before" and "after" shots, so they can see what the chemo is doing to your body.

That's when they found the fluid around my heart and the damage to my lungs from the radiation. But they also said I had taken longer to reach a 150 heartbeat than anybody they'd done, including a few marathon runners. That surprised me, since I had been feeling so tired at the end of the season.

I also needed a bone marrow test, and I wasn't looking forward to it. I just hated those. And this one was a core sample, with a needle that was about one-fourth inch in diameter and about four inches long. I guess I was getting used to it because it didn't hurt that badly. Or maybe Dr. Wolf just had some sharper needles, because he didn't have to pound on me.

I was still getting ready for chemo. I had a catheter put in, which I recommend to anybody who needs intravenous treatments. It's easier and it saves a lot of anxiety, wondering if they'll find a vein to shoot the chemo into you.

Another advantage to a catheter is that it lets you stick closer to your cycle. If they can't find a vein, it can throw your treatment off.

Dr. Wolf recommended a Broviac. I didn't ask a lot of questions. I just knew there'd be a tube coming out of my chest. The downside is that if you get an infection there, it can kill you. Everybody I've talked to who's had it both ways says the catheter is much, much easier. I can't stress that enough.

I had surgery for the Broviac, a tubing that goes under the skin up near the collarbone and into a vein. Outside, the tubing exits the skin about three inches below the collarbone and hangs down to the belt line. Halfway down, it splits into two leads, each with a yellow "port" that accepts the needles.

The surgery was supposed to mean an overnight stay, but I was worried because Heidi was ready to give birth any day. I didn't want to be in the hospital when I'd promised her I'd be there when the baby was born.

But it worked out. Heidi's dad took me in and when she came to visit me with our friends Jay and Dorothy Ferriera, the surgery was over. Then one of the nurses came in and said if I learned how to take care of the Broviac and keep it clean, I could leave that night.

I took a crash course in changing the bandages three times a week, wiping the skin and the catheter with alcohol, putting on an antibacterial ointment and putting two bandages on top of the incisions, being careful not to breathe into the open wound and risk an infection. I also found out I had to take a syringe and inject an anti-coagulant into the lines every day, to make sure the blood wouldn't clot in them and they'd stay clear.

Heidi and our friends ended up taking me home.

It was getting harder to keep the secret. On January 4, we'd gone to the Jimmy DiGisi Basketball Game at Northern Highlands High School in Allendale, New Jersey. It's a fund-raiser for Tomorrow's Children, run by two of the founders of TCF in honor of their son who had died of cancer.

I'd gone for four years and I always gave a talk at half time. I'd welcome everyone, then talk about my Hodgkin's. But this time, we'd learned I was sick again. We didn't want to tell anybody, but I couldn't lie to some of those people. So while I was talking to the crowd, Heidi was in the stands, telling David Jurist, the co-president of Tomorrow's Children, and Lynn Hoffman, the director.

It was one of the hardest talks I ever gave. I thought about not going, but I had to be there. It was too important to those people and too important to me. But I couldn't say I was sick again, so I just told everyone about the great things in cancer treatment and that people can be cured. I didn't say I was doing great because I didn't want to lie.

We couldn't keep it secret much longer. On January 7, a reporter called Jack Mills, my football agent, and said he knew something was going on with me. Another reporter called George Young, the Giants general manager, and George told him to sit on the story.

We knew that we'd have to have a press conference to spell out the situation. I'd let them ask any questions they wanted, and then I'd ask them to leave me alone.

We learned from our mistakes, and we wanted to control things this time.

We decided to have the press conference on Tuesday, January 10. Of course, it leaked. The guy who had been sitting on the story at Young's request had to go with it. And once he let it out, it was everywhere. The story was in all the papers Tuesday, even before I talked to the press at Giants Stadium.

The press conference went smoothly. I went through the process. I was calm and rational, I wasn't emotional or anything like that. And I told them, "As soon as I'm done here, I'm going in to have my first chemo treatment. And my wife is expecting a baby." I made myself available for as long as they needed me, then I asked them to please give us some time to ourselves.

Then I got into a limo and headed for Manhattan and the brave new world of chemotherapy.

Chapter 12
Cycles

I rode to Dr. Wolf's office, 115 East 61st Street in Manhattan, and this time, I didn't know what to expect. It was all brand new to me.

I was sitting on a table in one of his examination rooms, and he walked in with a tray loaded with syringes full of the drugs.

He took the first syringe, screwed it into the catheter port and—zip!—shot it right in.

That was the nitrogen mustard. Originally, the stuff had been developed by the Army as a chemical weapon, an offshoot of the mustard gas used in World War I. Now, the weapon was going to save my life.

Suddenly, I got a mustard taste in my mouth and up my nose. A coldness went through my body, like ice hitting my veins. It wasn't a chilling cold, but I could feel it. I don't know if it was psychosomatic, but—they were putting some weird stuff in me.

Then, Dr. Wolf screwed in the next syringe, and shot me full of oncovin. With that one, I got a tinfoil taste in my mouth and broke into a cold sweat. My stomach got queasy and I got a dull headache. But he'd given me two Compazine tablets to settle me down before he'd started, so it wasn't too bad.

The mustard and the oncovin were the first parts of the treatment plan, what they called "MOPP-ABV." Each letter stands for another chemical killer they're using to attack the cancer.

"M" is for mustard. "O" is for oncovin. I also got prednisone and procarbazine tablets to take orally. That's the P and P. ABV is for adriamycin, bleomycin, and velban. I'd be getting those later in the cycle.

That first day, I got my two intravenous drugs and my pills.

Then I got back in the limo and went home. That was one of the nice things the Giants did for me. With the radiation, there weren't any serious immediate side effects, so I'd drive in myself. But with chemo, you really shouldn't be behind the wheel. You need a friend there, or a car service. There are groups, like Cancer Care, who will arrange transportation to and from the treatment, or sometimes the hospital will do it. I was lucky, I had the Giants to take care of it.

I had that first treatment on January 10, the day of my press conference at Giants Stadium.

Lyndsay was born January 12.

Heidi had started having contractions the Sunday before, and she was just praying the baby would be born before I started my treatments.

That didn't happen. She was having contractions off and on while I was at the press conference and getting my first treatment. I kept calling her to check, but they never got regular enough to go to the hospital. They were probably brought on by the stress.

On Wednesday morning, the day after my first treatment, we went to see Heidi's doctor and they hooked her up to a monitor. They decided that they would induce labor the next day if nothing happened, but the contractions started again Wednesday afternoon. I got about three hours' sleep that night and Heidi got none. We went to the hospital at four o'clock in the morning. Lyndsay was born five hours later.

Lyndsay is the baby we weren't supposed to have. She was like a special gift. But Heidi's emotions were all mixed up.

"I've got this baby," she'd say, "but cancer is taking my husband. The person I love isn't going to be with me, and someone I didn't even ask for will be. At that moment, and I know it sounds terrible to say, I didn't want her. Can you understand that?"

I could. After the radiation, they thought I was going to be sterile. And when we found out Heidi was pregnant, one of my big concerns was if the baby would have two arms, two legs, 10 fingers, 10 toes. I was worried about the side effects of the radiation. We never talked about it and the doctors downplayed it, but I was still worried. I think we both were.

Lyndsay was smaller than Brittany was when she was born. Lyndsay is my little peanut. I don't know if that had anything to do with the radiation, or it's just genetics and the luck of the draw. But she wasn't as big. And she wasn't as beautiful.

Brittany was just a beautiful, pink baby, a perfect baby. Lyndsay was a little blue, and she was kind of scratched up, and her head was cone-shaped when she was born. She wasn't beautiful instantly, the way Brittany was.

But she's beautiful now. The two have totally different personalities, but I guess that's common. They're both smart kids, though. And we love them both.

In spite of what I'd asked, a few reporters came to the hospital when Lyndsay was born. But that was nice, because her name made all the papers, even though every single one of them misspelled it.

It was like life and death. We had a new baby, a new life. Now I was ready to fight for mine.

My treatment was set up on a 28-day cycle. On Day 1, I went in for the MOPP, taking the mustard and the oncovin by the catheter, and the procarbazine and prednisone pills daily. I was chugging pills morning, noon, and night. I had to get a pill caddy to remember what I'd taken and when. Every Sunday night, I'd fill up my pill caddy and then just go through it until the next Sunday night.

Day 8, I went back for the ABV, and kept taking the prednisone pills for a week. Days 15 to 28, I was off. But days 15 to 21 my white blood count would take a nose dive. A normal white count is between 10,000 and 14,000. Once, mine got down to 200. Since the white cells are the ones that fight off infections, that meant I was in serious danger of losing a battle with my body's own natural bacteria, and I'd have to be quarantined at home or, if the white count was too low and I started running a fever, I'd have to go into the hospital.

Once I got through that, I had about six good days before the cycle started all over again.

There were other side effects, too. One of the drugs made my sinuses flush out right away, and I'd have to have a wad of tissues ready every time Dr. Wolf shot it in. Another of them gave me a taste of baking soda. The problem there was that it wasn't a pleasant association. Baking soda is used as a common cleanser, especially in limousines. Every time Harold, the driver the Giants' service sent for me, would pick me up, my stomach would start churning, and I'd have to roll down the window and stick my head out, like some shaggy dog.

Smells were always a problem, just like that smell in the radiation unit at Sloan-Kettering. After a while, the smell of the alcohol wipes I had to use every day to clean the Broviac started to make me gag. It wasn't anything physical. It was more mental from the direct association with the chemo.

Dr. Wolf is very thorough. Sometimes, I think he tells too much. When he explained the chemo to Heidi and me, and I asked him about the side effects, he listed about 20: liver failure, kidney failure, heart problems, lung problems, numbness in hands and feet, loss of hair. He said, "I could go on. Now, you might have some of these and you might have none."

I guess I'm the kind of guy who just wanted to know a few.

The treatments started with the MOPP. That didn't bother me as much as the ABV. I'd come home after getting the treatments and feel like I had the flu for the next two days. So I'd sit in my red leather chair in the family room, just zonked out.

I'd lose my sense of taste. It came back in a couple of days after the first cycle, though it took longer and longer every cycle. To counter that, I'd drink Bacardi mixers straight, without water or alcohol added, just ice. So the taste was very strong. I drank a lot of high-calorie shakes to keep my weight up, but needed something with a really strong flavor to it, just to get some satisfaction. It's hard to eat when you can't taste anything. Everything is bland, even beyond bland. The frustrating part for Heidi was that she's an incredible cook. She'd still make great meals, but I couldn't appreciate them. (At least the babysitter ate well.)

It wasn't just the loss of taste. Certain foods would make me ill. For a while, it was strawberry yogurt. Then, toward the end, there was a growing list of things that triggered it. I don't know if it was psychological or physiological. It didn't really matter. If something turns your stomach, you're sick.

On Day 8, the ABV hit harder. Right away, I got some tingling in my fingers and in my feet. It was mild, and they'd said it could happen. But it would get worse.

I began waking up and not being able to get back to sleep. That was from the prednisone. It just wired me up like you can't believe. I'd sleep for two hours, then be up for an hour and a half. It'd take half of a sleeping pill to get back to sleep, then I'd wake up after another two hours, take another half of a pill, and be out two more hours. While I was up, I'd feed Lyndsay. Or I'd read a book. I'm not a TV watcher. Besides, there's nothing on at that hour, except maybe "Nick at Night."

If I was up at six o'clock, I knew I wouldn't be able to get back to sleep, so I'd head down to the stadium with the sun coming up to start my workout. I figured since it was already light out, I might as well do something.

On Day 15, my white count would drop. That first time, it went down to 1,000. That's when I had my biggest problem with the treatments.

It was January 24, a Tuesday afternoon, and I was lying in bed, curled up in the fetal position. I felt like someone had kicked me in the groin. The pain was so bad I was in tears. It was the only time I ever broke down and cried.

I looked up at Heidi and said, "If it's going to be like this every time, I don't know if I can go through this."

That's the only time I ever said that. It's the only time I ever cried, the only time I remember crying since I was little. It was just incredible pain.

Heidi didn't know what to do. She just sat there and held me.

"What do you do when a man starts crying?" she says now. "I wanted you to cry, but when you did I didn't know what to do. I've always wanted you to open up to me, and you never had. Then when you did, it was like a dam breaking and I felt worse because there was absolutely nothing I could do."

It felt good to cry. It had been a long time since I had. It's not like I was wailing like a baby. It was a calm kind of crying. It didn't help the pain much, but it helped enough to take the edge off.

Heidi's explanation is that it was the first time in my life that I couldn't do anything to control what was going on. No matter what I did, I was going to be in pain.

And she said the way I felt at that minute was the way she felt through the whole chemotherapy.

That day, we called Dr. Wolf and he sent us to Pascack Valley Hospital in New Jersey. He had never heard of anything like it before. He talked to other doctors and none of them had ever heard of anything like it.

Dr. Wolf wanted me to go into New York, but I couldn't even stand up straight, I had to walk hunched over. So I told him I'd go to Pascack Valley. Dr. Allan Levy, one of the Giants' team doctors, was there, and I knew he'd get whatever specialist I needed.

Levy said nothing showed up in my bladder and kidneys. "You may have some type of infection that we can't see or sense," he said. So they gave me an antibiotic.

My white count was down to 700, which put me in quarantine at my house. I shouldn't have gone to Pascack Valley, but if I'd had an untreated infection, it could have been deadly. I had to have somebody look at me, and I had to have somebody close to home.

They never really found out what it was. The pain would start slowly and build up, and then stay constant, just never going away.

I used my usual cure, ice. I was icing my groin three times a day. And I was taking Tylenol with codeine. By Thursday, it started easing up a little bit.

All those side effects Dr. Wolf warned me about, and the worst was the one he hadn't expected.

He told me there would be at least six cycles, six months of treatments. But he originally had told me 20 radiation treatments, too, then added 20 more in the abdomen "just to be sure."

I thought I could plan out my whole six months of chemotherapy. I'd know when I could do speaking engagements and when I couldn't. Dr. Wolf and Heidi both were trying to tell me I might not be able to stick to the schedule, but that's not the way I think.

The first week of a cycle wasn't bad. Toward the end of that week, I was starting to get edgy from the prednisone. Then I'd get the ABV and feel awful for two or three days. But by Day 11 or 12, I'd try to get out and work out at the stadium. In the third week, my white count would go down, and I'd be in quarantine. That's the week I couldn't do any speaking engagements. Then I'd have one "good" week a month, the last week of the cycle. At least I was semi-functional around the house.

One of the things that bothered me was that we had just had the baby and here I was, another baby in the house. That's what I was at least two of the four weeks. I'd sit downstairs in my red leather chair, like a zombie.

Heidi hadn't said anything during the first cycle. She thought this was the way it was supposed to be. She thought I'd get used to it. But in the second cycle, Dr. Wolf asked her, "How is he handling it?"

She said, "He isn't."

Dr. Wolf had told me he'd give me enough chemo for my body size and maybe a little bit more. Then if I was handling it, he'd increase the doses.

Only Heidi was right, I wasn't handling it.

I was just sitting in that chair, with my eyes bulged and my pupils dilated. My skin had a gray hue to it. I wasn't sleeping at night, so I was taking a lot of naps in the day. Sleep was precious to me and everybody in the house tiptoed around.

Dr. Wolf made the adjustments. He had been giving me the higher doses because of my size. In the third cycle, after Heidi had told him what was going on, he cut down the mustard. In the fifth, he cut down the mustard and the oncovin. In the sixth, he cut the oncivin even more and in the seventh, cut it out completely.

That was to ward off one of oncovin's side effects, the numbing in my hands and feet. By then they had become useless.

Dr. Wolf explained that Dr. Vincent DeVita, the man who developed the MOPP treatment in the 1960s, felt very strongly that the drugs shouldn't be cut back in order to produce the optimal cure. And Dr. Wolf knew I wanted him to treat me as intensely as possible, to make sure that there wouldn't be any third time for my cancer. But he had to weigh that against the possible loss of the use of my hands and feet, permanently. And he made the call.

There were some side effects, though, that he couldn't do anything about. Like the constipation.

I'll try to put this delicately. I had problems in the bathroom. The chemo attacks the mucus cells, and there's not enough fluid in the bowels to keep the stool soft. I remember talking to Alex, one of the kids at Tomorrow's Children, and he had terrible problems with it. It got to where his parents would go in the bathroom with him and hold his hand and encourage him.

Normally, I'm as regular as clockwork, but with the chemo, I became constipated.

That's one of the problems nobody talks about, and I guess you understand why. They'd rather talk about your hair.

I started losing mine around Day 20 of my first cycle. It started slowly, but pretty soon I'd take a shower and wash my hair, and my hands would be covered with fur, like a werewolf.

I was going to the Dapper Dan charity dinner in Pittsburgh on February 4 and the big concern was whether I'd have any hair left. It was just coming out in clumps. I started to wash it every third day, hoping it would hold up. I just didn't want to go to Pittsburgh bald, and I didn't want to wear a hairpiece.

It held on. And it was a great dinner. I sat between Mean Joe Greene and Mike Webster, the former Pittsburgh Steelers. And that's where I met Mario Lemieux of the Penguins. He was Dapper Dan's "Man of the Year." Nobody knew then that he would come down with Hodgkin's four years later.

It was about a week later that I gave Heidi one of the shocks of her life.

I shaved my mustache.

I was tired of having it fall out in my food. But it was like losing a friend. I'd had it since I was a sophomore in college. Heidi didn't even know what I looked like without it. I shaved it off, real slow. Then I stood staring at the mirror, trying to decide if I'd done the right thing. Without that mustache, I'm just not a good-looking guy.

I went downstairs and Heidi was outside. She walked in the door, took one look at me, and walked right out again.

She composed herself, then came back in and said, "Don't ever do that to me again. It's not funny. Do you know what it's like to come into your house and see a stranger standing there?"

It was a sign of things to come.

Then one day I was working out at Giants Stadium and I was starting to think I'd look better without hair than with the hair I had. I read a story about the late Jim Valvano, the basketball coach who won an NCAA title with North Carolina State. When he was undergoing chemo treatments, he decided to shave his head. It was his way of saying he was still in charge, that he would make the decision on whether he had hair or not. But his hair grew back. He just wasn't hit with that side effect.

I was making a choice, too. I told Mike Ryan to get an electric shaver and just cut it down to one-fourth inch. But that looked horrible, so I told him to take it down to scalp level.

While Mike was clipping, Parcells walked by. I couldn't really see him, until I caught him in the mirror. He had this stunned look on his face, like he was in shock. I think that's when it really hit him I was going through some pretty serious stuff.

I was sitting there with my face bloated and my skin gray. I had no mustache and, now, no hair. Bill watched for two or three minutes and then just walked away.

I thought it was all right, but Heidi said that with no hair, my head was a constant reminder that I was sick.

"Every time I look at you without hair," she said, "it's like I see a tattoo saying 'cancer' across your forehead. With the hairpiece, it will just look like you have a bad toupee."

So I finally caved in and we shopped for a hairpiece. They're pretty expensive. Insurance paid $250 towards one, but for that you'll get a piece of steel wool to put on your head.

Here's a tip: If you're going to get one, pick it out when your hair starts falling out so you get the right color and the right hair style, and you don't have to do it from a picture.

The hairpiece confused Brittany, who was three. It was Daddy with hair, Daddy without hair. But Lyndsay would just look at me and start laughing. I guess she was saying, "Ha, ha, Daddy. I've got more hair than you do and I don't have very much." Later on, when my hair started growing back, it was like a contest, to see when I would finally surpass Lyndsay.

But I didn't wear the hairpiece all the time. And I was shaving my head because it was more comfortable than putting it over stubble. One day I was down at Giants Stadium working out and I didn't have my hair on or my mustache and I was all bloated. All of our scouts walked by and none of them said hello. They had no idea who I was.

I was still working out, trying to keep a piece of football. It was a way I could gauge how far down I was going. Cleans had always been my best lift, but my hands and feet were so bad I had no balance, and I couldn't clean the bar up to my chest. So I was doing clean-pulls, which is like a dead lift, just raising the bar up to a standing position.

When I had been in great shape, I'd do a clean-pull at 450 pounds. Then I went down to 315. Each week, I'd try to maintain what I did the week before, but I dropped down to 235. And to get those, when my feet got bad, I had to scrape the bar up my legs, so my shins were bleeding.

I'd work out at Giants Stadium and shower there. Initially, they'd told me not to get the Broviac wet, and I'd put plastic covers on it whenever I showered. But another doctor told me I only had to do that until the skin healed around the tube. Then I could shower, or even go swimming.

Once, Bill saw me in the shower. It was the first time he had seen the Broviac tubes coming out of my chest. He just stared at me, again, with no idea what to say. I tried to joke with him about it, but he wasn't going to be joked with. He had a hard time seeing me go downhill. He really did.

I had to be careful down at the stadium. I used my own bar of soap to avoid bacteria. And I had to have all my prep stuff for my catheter. I was just trying to keep a routine. Then, on February 22, I hit a crisis.

It was a Monday in the third week of my second cycle and

my white count was dropping. I had gone to see Dr. Wolf and it had come in at 500, and I had a fever of 100 degrees.

He sent me into his office. I waited for him, expecting him to tell me I had to quarantine at home for a week. But he sat down and said, "Karl we have a problem. You're running a fever and your white count is 500. With your spleen out, your body has no defense. So I'm going to have to put you in the hospital."

"What? What are you talking about?"

"You have to go in the hospital and get some antibiotics," he said. "And it's very important that you do it quickly because it's very dangerous for you at this point. I want to put you in New York Hospital right now."

I didn't want to. There was no way I wanted Heidi to have to leave the kids in New Jersey to visit me in New York every day.

"That's not going to work," I said. "Can I go to Pascack Valley?"

"I don't know anybody there," Dr. Wolf said. "I don't know what kind of treatment you would get."

But I pleaded with him. I had him call Dr. Levy and he gave us the name of Dr. David Israel, an oncologist at Pascack Valley. Dr. Wolf spoke to Dr. Israel and became comfortable enough to have Dr. Israel take care of me.

I took my limo home and Heidi was frantic. Dr. Wolf had told her he'd once seen a patient who started running a fever and was dead three hours later. When I got home, she ran around and got my stuff together and I was out the door in 15 minutes.

I got to the hospital at five-thirty. Heidi got there at six. Then we sat and waited.

Dr. Wolf had called ahead to make sure the antibiotics were there, but at seven o'clock, I still hadn't been hooked up. So Heidi went a little crazy. She thought there was a chance I could die, because that's what she'd heard Dr. Wolf tell her.

I had rushed over there so they could start immediately. When your white count is below 1,000, the body has no defense, even against the bacteria that your body normally has. That's why you run a fever. If you get a real infection, there's nothing to stop it. And that's where you really get in trouble.

It'd be another case of not dying from the cancer, but dying from the treatments. My count was so low a common cold could have killed me. Researchers are coming out with new medications now that are extremely expensive but will keep your white count up when you're going through chemo. I've talked to a couple of people who have had them and they say they're great.

I just sat there for three hours, waiting for my antibiotics. And I finally got them around eight o'clock. The next day, several people, including Dr. Israel, did some big-time apologizing.

Once they got my IV going, it was pretty uneventful. They'd come in to check my temperature every four hours. I was very tired. I read, slept, and watched TV. Every night, Heidi would bring me dinner from Finnegan's.

After five days, I got to go home.

That crisis was over. The next one was just around the corner.

Chapter 13
Homecoming

It was April Fools' Day, but it was no joke.

We were walking through O'Hare Airport in Chicago. Heidi was just a couple of steps behind me with the kids, and she was thinking, He can't walk. His feet are numb, and he just flips them out in front of him. His hips shake every time he takes a step. He's bloated like a balloon, with rolls of stomach hanging over his pants. His face is gray, the color completely gone. He's wearing a bad toupee. I don't know this person. He isn't the man I married.

We were back in Illinois visiting my parents for the first time since I'd started chemo.

I don't want to be here, Heidi thought. I don't want to be in this situation. I want out.

She thought about leaving me, but she wouldn't and couldn't do it.

I didn't know it was that bad. She never told me. I was just focused on taking my treatments, on fighting the cancer and getting well. I really didn't think about what it was doing to her.

"For the first time since we'd met, Karl's family wasn't jealous of me," Heidi said. "When they saw him, they were shocked. Very, very shocked. And he was going to get worse. I had to make a decision about whether I was going to stay with him and deal with the situation, or whether I'd just get out."

She stayed. Our babysitter, a 19-year-old German girl named Petra Schadt, became Heidi's lifeline. Petra was her best friend, from the time they woke up until the time they went to bed. Heidi needed someone to talk to. She couldn't talk to me, not about this. So she talked to Petra.

Heidi never felt guilty about what she'd been thinking. "I know if I were going through it, Karl would be there for me," she explained. "But not to the degree that I was there for him. I was living for this person who was sick, and I didn't know if he was going to live or die, leaving me alone with two children. And I was only 26 years old, and that's too young to be dealing with all this."

The treatments can be harder on the support person than on the patient. I knew what I had to do. Heidi didn't. She didn't know what she was supposed to do to make me feel better, to help me, to comfort me. And I wasn't exactly telling her.

And while that was going on between Heidi and me, we had to deal with my family.

When we got to DeKalb, everyone tried to act as normal as they could, but there was tension.

To start, there were too many of us there. Heidi and I and the kids. My grandparents, and my brother and sister and their families. We definitely reached critical mass.

There were no heart-to-heart talks, no real communications with anybody. Everything was on the surface. It seemed like nobody in my family could say the word "cancer." They just tried to ignore it.

My dad, for instance, just never shows his emotions. He grew up in a different generation, when the men went out and worked and the women stayed at home with the kids. My dad never changed a diaper. But he was there for every baseball game and every basketball game we played. He had been a veterinarian, and one of the reasons he changed jobs was to be able to take off and watch his kids play. He became a stockbroker, so he wasn't on call and could take an afternoon here and there to watch a sixth-grade basketball game.

We'd communicate through sports. Even today, most of our conversations are about the Giants.

My mom asked some questions about the treatments. She wanted to know. My dad did, too, but he just doesn't ask.

Basically, they reacted the way I reacted. No denial, no depression, just get on with it. That's how we were brought up.

Our inability to communicate caused a little discomfort, though, because they really did want to know what was going on. Heidi was the one who had to tell them things, and they didn't want to believe her. So it just caused problems. It would have been a lot better if I'd just been able to open up—if I'd been brought up to be that way.

We got there Saturday and went to a cousin's wedding reception. I really didn't want to go, because it had been the first extensive walking I'd done and my feet were really killing me. I did it because everybody expected me to do it, and I always do what's expected. It was just a very long day.

Back home Sunday, I got to see my family, but it wasn't a great experience. It was just too crowded, with 10 adults and six kids. My sister Karen and my brother Kevin were there with their families, but I didn't get to spend much time with any of them. That bothered them and made things pretty tense. After two days, my dad had had enough and so had we. My sister wanted to stay past the weekend, but my dad told her to go back to Milwaukee with her family because the whole situation was just out of control.

We stayed in Illinois until Wednesday and then headed home.

Before we'd left New Jersey, life was starting to become more routine. Once I'd gone through two cycles, I had a feeling of what to expect. But I still had to run through a battery of tests.

One of the tests was a CAT scan at New York Hospital. They had pumped me full of liquids, about a gallon total, and started the scan. Once you start one of those tests, you can't stop, and all of a sudden I knew that what had gone in had to come out. I told them, "If we don't hurry up, something's going to happen that hasn't happened to me since I was a very little kid." My brain was floating, and as soon as we stopped and they unhooked me, I ran for the bathroom. Made it, too.

Toward the end of my second cycle, after I'd been quarantined in the hospital when my count dropped, I was told that because my count was so low, they were going to put off my bone marrow harvest. That's a procedure to collect your marrow and store it, in case you need to use it later. Anyway, they wanted to put it off for four days and I was very upset. My schedule, remember.

On March 9, I went in for the harvest. I had it done at Sloan-Kettering and that made two full cycles of "ring around the hospitals." I'd started at the Hospital for Special Surgery for my shoulder, the operation I didn't have. Then I'd gone underground and across the street to New York Hospital for the thoracotomy and laparotomy. Then it was over to Sloan for the radiation.

And finally, I'd gone back to Special Surgery to get my shoulder done. Then to New York Hospital to have the lump taken out and the Broviac put in. Now I was back at Sloan for the bone marrow harvest.

For the harvest, the doctor punched 24 holes in my hips,

and, as you can imagine, I was very sore! It hurt to move, hurt to sit, hurt to do anything. And they'd put some stretch tape around my hips. When I took that off, the skin came with it.

It took four or five days for the soreness to go away, and longer for the skin to heal. (While on chemo, those poisons are killing the skin cells, so it takes forever to heal.)

I had the marrow harvest done, then I went in for Day 1 of my third cycle on Thursday. My white count was still low, though, and I had to talk Dr. Wolf into starting the treatments.

"Listen, we're already off four days," I told him. "We've got some things planned and we can't screw it up."

We were taking our first trip since I'd started chemo, down to Baltimore for the Ed Block Awards dinner that Monday. It was like a test run to see if I'd be ready to travel to Illinois.

So I got the MOPP. Dr. Wolf decreased the dosages a little, and I was getting a little used to it, too. My body was handling it better and I didn't just sit there like a zombie in my red leather chair. In fact, we went to the circus.

Brittany's birthday was two days away, so that night we took her to the Ringling Brothers circus at the Meadowlands. Vic Del Guercio, the Giants director of special projects, got us into a suite at the arena. It's not really the best place to watch a circus, being a little far away. But when you're with a 3-year-old who's bouncing off the walls, it was nice. I was a little concerned that with my count down and getting treatment that day, I'd be pushing it a little too much, but I was really okay.

Sunday, we had Brittany's birthday party, just adults and no kiddies. And the next day, we flew to Baltimore for the Block Awards.

It was a wild trip. We flew out of Westchester County Airport in White Plains, New York down to Washington. Then we took a helicopter over to Baltimore. It was my first time in a helicopter, and I had to fold myself up just to get in the door. There wasn't an inch to spare and Garan Veris of the New England Patriots, who had flown down with us from White Plains, had to wait for a car to drive him while we went on a sky tour of Washington and all the monuments. It was really a beautiful trip. But overall, it took us six hours to get from White Plains to our hotel. The guys from the Buffalo Bills drove down, and it only took them seven.

Ed Block was the trainer for the Baltimore Colts for 23 years, and his foundation raises money to help abused children. Tuesday afternoon, I went over to the house where some of them stay. One kid just wanted to sit on my lap and hold my hand. He got really attached to me. It was a great day, really kind of special.

While I was there, Heidi went shopping and relaxed. It was her first chance to get away from the kids and from everything else. It was great for her and I think she needed it badly.

I looked very bad, of course. My face was puffy and my skin was gray, but nobody said a thing. And Tuesday night was a great affair.

The Block Awards go to one player from each NFL team who has shown courage in coming back from some type of injury or illness to make a contribution to his team.

I sat next to Doug Williams, the quarterback from the Washington Redskins who had just been named the Most Valuable Player in Super Bowl XXII. Talk about how the NFL can treat a guy like dirt! You just had to hear his story. He had been drafted by Tampa Bay and had taken them to the playoffs, and was negotiating a new contract. His wife had just died and he had been left alone to raise a two-year-old daughter. About that time Hugh Culverhouse, the Buccaneers owner, offered him about two-thirds of what Doug felt he should be getting. It was a take-it-or-leave-it situation, and Williams left. He had no plans, and no other NFL team would touch him. He went to the USFL's Oklahoma Outlaws and then came back with the Redskins and wound up as the first black quarterback to win a Super Bowl.

His story made me glad to be with an organization like the Giants. There are others that don't treat the players as well. In fact, the Redskins later burned Doug, too, cutting him loose when they thought Jay Schroeder was a hotter prospect.

Overall, it was a great night. I think I got the biggest applause of anybody. And the trophy is the most beautiful one I have. I keep most of my awards down in my basement, but that one is displayed right up in the family room. It's the one I just absolutely love.

That trip was a great experience for Heidi and me. It was our first real break from the chemo and the cancer.

We came back on Wednesday, March 15, and the next Monday we hosted a St. Patrick's Day party for Tomorrow's Children at Hackensack Medical Center, along with the other Giants' wives.

It was good to sign some autographs and see the kids. I can't tell you how much they meant to me, meant to both of us.

There was a boy there named Alex, with a type of bone cancer, and he'd had parts of the muscles of his legs removed. But every time I'd see him he'd just smile big and say, "Doing great!"

I've met so many inspirational kids. Michael Gillick is another one. We didn't hook up through Tomorrow's Children. I just met him down at Giants Stadium when someone brought him there. When Michael was born, the doctors didn't think he'd live two months. He's 14 years old now.

Michael has had tumors in his brain that caused blindness in one eye and impaired vision in the other. He's had tumors in his back that actually broke his spine. Sometimes, when I haven't spoken to him in a few weeks, I am afraid to call him, expecting to hear bad news. But he has been a pillar of strength for me. He's just an incredible little boy.

These are the kids you talk to. When getting radiation, I'd see other people in the waiting room, people who held their dignity while their bodies were falling apart. Or I'd talk to Jeff Blatnick, who had been through it.

But with chemo, there wasn't a chance to get to know other patients. I would go to Dr. Wolf's office, take my treatments and go home.

I liked to talk to the kids. I helped them, but they also gave me strength. Children are remarkable. Sometimes they can handle the treatments better than adults because they don't question the treatment— it's what they have to do.

Michael Gillick doesn't know what it's like to have a normal childhood. But he's doing as well as he can. When you see what these kids are going through and how well they are handling it, how can you not fight through what's happening to you?

I had side effects I could live with. On March 17, I took the second treatment of my third cycle, the ABV, and I started to gag. Just thinking about it, I'd start to gag. It was getting harder to put those things into my body, even the heparin lock, the anticoagulant that kept the blood out of the Broviac.

My hands were starting to get really bad. It was hard to write. My thumb was the worst. I couldn't control it. Both hands were tingling, and sometimes this sensation would travel up into the forearms. Buttoning shirts was getting harder. Tying my shoes became a challenge.

I couldn't sleep at night, and I had a problem with near-blackouts during the day. Worst of all, my patience was gone, a side effect from the prednisone.

I snapped at Brittany for the smallest things. I'd fly off the handle, then get upset with myself for getting mad at her. Then I was more likely to jump at her again, which would make me even more upset.

It wasn't me, but the treatments were making me act that way. Not being in control upset me very much.

I wasn't myself anymore. When I looked in the mirror, I wasn't seeing myself. I saw a monster looking back. Heidi finally talked me into taking tranquilizers.

Life was very hard.

It was at that time that we went to Illinois, back home to my family.

So how could I not understand what Heidi was thinking when we were walking through that airport?

I was thinking the same things about myself.

Chapter 14
Going to Disney World

So, Karl Nelson, you're winning your fight against cancer. Where are you going now?

"I'm going to Disney World!"

We got back from Illinois on April 6, a Thursday. Heidi and I were both exhausted, physically and emotionally, from the trip. I was starting to feel more uncomfortable about my hair, my mustache, and my overall appearance. Every day, it bothered me more and more. And I've already told you how Heidi felt.

The next day, I started my fourth cycle.

I was complaining more and more about my hands and feet. I'd done more walking on the trip than I'd done before, and my feet were killing me. Dr. Wolf wanted to cut back on the drugs again and I fought him. I wanted to go hard one more time. I didn't want to mess up the treatments and risk another recurrence. I told him to keep hitting me, and for one more time anyway, he did.

Maybe I should have let him cut back then. My hands were cramping up all the time. I'd write and have to drop the pen and use my other hand to physically straighten my fingers.

Still, I was concerned about Disney World. You know, the place where all the Super Bowl MVP's say they're going.

We had a trip planned with the kids, and I wanted to know if there was anything I could do for my hands and feet. Turns out there wasn't a helluva lot.

Heidi told me to rent a motorized wheelchair, but my ego wouldn't let me do that. Dr. Wolf also warned me that I'd be hypersensitive to the sun. During radiation, I once went out to watch an afternoon practice in late October, and my neck got so badly burned that it blistered.

With radiation, you're only sensitive where it hits the skin.

With chemo, it's all over your body. So Dr. Wolf told me to use a strong sunblock every day. First, though, I had to spot-test all these products to see if I was allergic to any of their ingredients.

Nonetheless, I was really looking forward to that trip. Late in April, I had gone on tranquilizers. I was very down on myself then, and that was part of what Heidi had had a hard time dealing with. Heidi's the type of person who needs a challenge. One reason we have such a good relationship is that I don't love her to death, or cuddle her, or hold onto her or tell her I love her all the time. Because I'm not an open person, I keep her on her toes, fighting for my love. And she admits she needs that. She doesn't appreciate things that are handed to her.

But at this point, I was so down, and so dependent on her, that she didn't have that challenge. She was getting over what had troubled her in Illinois, too.

I was still in a funk, but I was working out at the stadium whenever I felt I could. I was trying to fight through it.

Maybe that's why I was looking forward to Florida. But I nearly blew the deal.

On April 22, a week before we were supposed to leave, I went to a retirement dinner for George Martin and Harry Carson, who'd left the Giants at the end of the '88 season. It was Day 15 of the fourth cycle and my white count was only 1,700. I shouldn't have gone, but because it was George and Harry, I had to be there.

The dinner was at the Norwood Manor in Norwood, New Jersey. During the cocktail hour, I stayed up in a private room, so I wouldn't have to see too many people. But the next day, I had a 100.8-degree fever. The day after, I wound up in the hospital.

I went in on Monday, April 24. We were going to Florida April 29. So I had to be out and I told the doctors that. I had a schedule and schedules are for keeping. We were doing a Cancer Survivors Day affair in Tampa that weekend, and we were going to see my grandparents. I wasn't going to miss it.

But my temperature shot up to 102 degrees. I got chills, then the sweats. By Thursday, I was still at 100 degrees and I only had one day left. Even worse, that night was our anniversary.

The first time I had to go to Pascack Valley (the time I had to wait nearly three hours for my antibiotics), I was put in one of their regular rooms. This time, I was in a suite. It had carpeted floors and a love seat and chairs around a coffee table. It had a 19-inch color television, and another TV by the bed. There were nice towels and a robe hanging in the bathroom. And it had a real menu with real choices—not that it mattered to a guy whose taste buds were being killed by chemo, but it was nicer for Heidi.

And that's where we had our "romantic" anniversary dinner. Don't get me wrong, the room was nice and the Giants were great to pick up the full tab, just like they always did any time I went into the hospital.

But as nice as the room was, it was still a hospital room. And I wanted out.

And I got out Friday. They didn't want to let me go, but I got them to put me on oral antibiotics instead of an IV. They were these "horse pill" things, but they said if I took them, I could go.

I knew once the white count had come back up, it meant I could beat off any bacteria in my body. If I got a real infection, it might not have been high enough, but I didn't think I was in a danger zone. We went home Friday afternoon to pack, and then left Saturday. So I looked at it like I had another 18 hours of recovery at home and that was enough. But we were definitely red-lining it.

We flew to Tampa on Saturday for a black-tie dinner that night. While we were in the airport, Heidi and I had another incident, more funny than serious this time.

I was facing the door, waiting for Heidi to come out of the ladies' room, and when she got out she just walked right past me. She was looking and looking and looking. She looked right at me. But she had no idea who I was.

"Heidi, it's me!"

But it really wasn't me. There was no way you could say that I was Karl Nelson right then. And the change happened in less than four months.

This time, though, we laughed it off. That night, we went to the dinner, and I had to wear my tux, which still fit even though I was fat and puffy. I had to borrow some studs from my grandfather because Heidi had forgotten to pack mine. She'd never worn a tux, so how was she to know?

At the dinner, I spoke just a few minutes—my standard speech. Dr. Anthony Ottiviani, who was sitting next to Heidi, pledged $69,000 to the cause, and he said it was because of my talk. He said, "If this man can fly all the way here from New Jersey while he's fighting this, then I can give you the money you need to reach your goal."

I guess they were ticked off that their goal wasn't $20,000 higher.

The next day, there was a picnic in Heritage Park. I met a lot of people there who had scars from different surgeries, who had lost limbs. It was pretty intense. They all had a common bond.

My talk that day was my "training camp" speech: The treatments are like camp, and you've got to go through them to get to the Super Bowl. Then we headed off for Disney World to meet Heidi's mom, Petra, and the kids, who'd flown directly to Orlando from New Jersey.

On Monday, May 1, we went to Disney World. We took the shuttle bus over from the Holiday Inn, and the plan was for me to stay until after lunch, then take Lyndsay back to the hotel, so we could both take naps. That first day, we took transportation around the park as much as we could, and I made it into the afternoon before we all headed back together.

It was great going to Disney World with the kids. I know this is hard for people who know me to believe, but it was very emotional for me, probably because of the treatments. That first day, we were sitting at "Bear Country Jamboree" and I had Lyndsay on my lap. She was just three-and-a-half months old and her eyes were open wide, taking in everything, and laughing. It was just so neat and tears welled up in my eyes. And that happened a few times, at "It's a Small World" and all the things the kids got a kick out of.

That first day I did all right. The next afternoon, I headed back at one o'clock with Lyndsay, leaving Heidi and her mother with Brittany in the park.

I walked to the handicapped parking area, where I'd been told the shuttle bus for our hotel would pick us up. I was going to catch the 1:15 p.m. bus and I had about five minutes to wait. When I got there, this guy in the booth said, "All the hotel buses are down there."

And he pointed about 200 yards away.

That might not sound very far, but my feet were so bad I could barely walk. And now I only had three minutes to get there.

I started walking as fast as I could, because I didn't want to miss it and have to wait an hour for the next shuttle. I was pushing Lyndsay's stroller and just throwing my feet out in front of me—Flop! Flop! Flop!—hoping I didn't step on something and twist my ankle or break my leg.

Finally, I got there and asked, "Which bus to the Holiday Inn?"

Another guy told me, "These buses go to the Disney hotels. The bus you want is back there."

And he pointed 200 yards back the way I came.

Luckily, he saw I had problems. I didn't have my hair on, and I was sweating and couldn't walk. So he relayed a call to the bus and had it hold until I got back. I'd had to go an extra 400 yards, and that was like walking 400 miles.

They had very nice motorized wheelchairs there. I just wouldn't use them, even though it would have been easier on all of us. When you're six feet, six inches, 265 pounds, and a professional football player, they're kind of geeky. You don't want to admit that you need a motorized chair to get around a kids' park. It is tough on the ego. My ego held up only until Thursday, however, when I couldn't walk anymore.

It was our last day and we were visiting Sea World. I broke down and we rented one of the chairs for $20, and it was worth the money. Then, at the Shamu show, I parked next to a boy, 10 or 12 years old, on a cart, too. He didn't have any hair either. We didn't say a word. We just both knew what was going on. He looked at me, I looked at him. I nodded my head at him, he nodded back. It's hard to describe all the thoughts going back and forth in just that little shake of the head. We didn't need to say anything.

I think we were saying, "It isn't easy, but we're going to make it."

That night, we flew home. It had been a nice change of scenery. Even though I looked like hell and felt a lot worse, it was somehow very refreshing to be able to see the kids enjoy the rides and attractions. It was important to me.

But it wasn't any big personal revelation. It didn't make me suddenly appreciate my life or theirs. I always knew I'd make it. I never thought I was going to die. I didn't need Disney World to turn that corner.

The next day, I started my fifth cycle.

The trip, in fact, might have cost me an extra cycle. When I had a CAT scan during that fifth cycle, it came up clean. Dr. Wolf had told me he wanted to go two cycles after the first clean scan.

I should have been happy. This was good news. But I was very upset. Because we were in Florida, I hadn't gotten a CAT scan before that fifth cycle. If I had, and it had come up clean,

I would have finished at six cycles. Now, I'd need a seventh.

Looking back now, I know there's no guarantee that the CAT scan would have come back clean if it had been taken any earlier. But I knew it would have been. I knew.

It was good news, but I always knew everything was going to be fine. Now I had that extra cycle. I tried to talk Dr. Wolf into stopping after six. I had that number set in the back of my head. I was ready for six. This was the same thing that had happened when I thought I was done with radiation after 20 treatments and had another 20 tacked on.

On May 15, I came home and told Heidi that Dr. Wolf had gotten the clean scan, but that I was upset.

She said, "What are you, stupid?"

(That's what she always says.)

I should have been happy. I should have been the guy yelling, "I'm going to Disney World!"

But Disney World might have cost me that extra cycle and I was just mad.

Still, I guess that's when I started seeing the end of the tunnel. I had thought the end of the tunnel was closer, but it turned out that the light I'd been seeing was just a reflection. The real end was another 100 yards farther away.

But I could live, literally, with that.

Chapter 15
Homestretch

All I had to do was make it through this fifth cycle, then two more, and I'd be done.

I went about getting through it the way I'd always done, just by moving forward.

The Giants held a minicamp in the middle of May of '89, and I went down there one day, the last day. I had been quarantined at home again because my count was down, but I wanted to stop by and at least make an appearance.

I was going to coach with the Giants during the '89 season. That's what they'd asked me to do to earn my money.

Just before I'd started the chemo, George Young had talked to Jack Mills, my football agent, and we were told that even though they didn't have to pay me anything for the upcoming season except a $65,000 severance, they'd take care of me. We weren't sure what they'd do financially, but we didn't care. They had already been very good to us.

In April, the Giants had to make a decision about me, to stick with the NFL's rules. I met with George and he told me they wouldn't offer me a formal contract, because that would have to be for $275,000 under the NFL guidelines.

The whole thing didn't get settled until the first day of training camp in July. That's when I signed the contract. Originally, George was talking about something like $103,000, but they ended up paying me $135,000, which is almost half of what I'd made the year before when I was still playing.

I'd already told Jack that we'd take whatever they offered. What was I going to do, hold out? Maybe play some golf with LT while Jack drove a harder bargain?

The Giants were more than generous. But they asked if I'd do something to justify the money. So I started coaching, and I started in that minicamp.

I spoke with Bill about what I'd be doing. I knew that my hands and feet were so bad that I wouldn't be able to make it through two practices a day during camp. Even Karl Nelson had to face up to that.

Bill said that would be no problem. I also asked if I had to go to the coach's meetings, since I wasn't going to be involved in designing game plans. I could use their meeting time to work out and do whatever I had to do and then just work with the players in practice. Again, he had no problem with that.

It was good to have things to keep me busy. At home, I tried to put together a swing set for the kids, and there was a lot of hammering wooden pegs into small holes. My hands were shot and I had no strength left in them. But I tucked the thumb under my other fingers and kept going. I'd like to blame the side effects of the treatments for the way that swing set came out, but the truth is I've never been very good around the house anyway.

Once I got the swing set up, I worked on opening our pool. The first time I went swimming, my feet felt like two bags of sand attached to the ends of my legs, dragging through the water.

I just kept going and on June 2, I started my sixth cycle.

That was the first and last time I got sick, and I still haven't figured out why. It was the MOPP treatment, the one that usually did not bother me.

Maybe it was the rough ride home. Harold, our limo driver, had tried to avoid a tie-up on the FDR Drive and took the city streets north towards the George Washington Bridge. That made it a rougher trip. When I got home two hours after the treatment, I was sick.

I guess it wouldn't have been a real chemo experience if I hadn't gotten sick at least once. Now there are drugs to calm your stomach that I hear work much better. I hadn't been bothered much at all; I guess I was just lucky.

On June 4, a Sunday, we went to the Tomorrow's Children picnic at David Jurist's house in Watchung, New Jersey. It's an incredible place, with a huge house and swimming pool and a tennis court with bleachers. There's a small lake that he built with an island, and it's got a tree house with real glass windows and a real roof.

It was great to see the kids again. I didn't wear my hair that day, and when I saw that some of the kids who were swimming had Broviacs, I lifted up my shirt to show them mine. I just tried to let them know that I was just like they were and that I was going to make it, so they could, too.

But the side effects were adding up, especially the oncovin effect on my hands and feet. A couple of days after the picnic, I was walking in our front yard and stepped in a hole. My balance was so bad I just fell down. It was very embarrassing. Nobody saw me, but it was embarrassing, and frustrating. I couldn't even walk in my own front yard without falling down.

It's worse, though, for the kids in treatment. The pain gets so bad they don't want to walk. We had a friend whose daughter's feet got so bad that she had to be carried everywhere.

When the kids stop walking, their calves shorten up. Then it takes a lot of therapy to teach them to walk again.

I couldn't walk more than 25 feet without losing control of my feet. I'd just lift one and hope it landed flat, then lift the next one.

I got my next-to-last ABV treatment June 9. Then I flew up to Rochester, New York for a golf outing for Camp Good Days and Special Times.

I couldn't play. I couldn't grip a golf club. In fact, I couldn't even button my shirt. I was there in the locker room and I had to turn to the guy next to me and ask him for help.

"Listen," I said, "I know this sounds stupid, but I'm going through chemo and it takes the strength out of my hands. I can't do these buttons. Can you do 'em?"

He was real nice about it, but it was embarrassing to be a full-grown guy who couldn't dress himself. It was just one more example of my loss of control.

"It was just one more thing Karl had to live with," Heidi says now. "Just one more time someone else was in control. That was very hard for him to deal with—that I was the one doing most of the charity work, taking care of the house and everything. Luckily we had enough money to have someone here to help me."

Sometimes, of course, we both needed help.

When I got back from Rochester, I went right to Giants Stadium to work out. While there, I got an emergency call from Heidi.

She had been upstairs getting dressed when Brittany walked into the room and asked, "Mommy, why is all that water in the basement?"

We'd hired a friend to paint the house for us, and he was using a power washer to get it ready. Somehow, he burst one of the pipes in our basement and caused a flood.

Heidi flew down the stairs and when she saw the nine inches of water covering the floor, she just started laughing. But Bruno Tavaroni, our friend, was terrified.

"Karl's going to shoot me!"

But Heidi couldn't stop laughing.

"If I didn't laugh, I'd cry," she said. "Everything that could have gone wrong had gone wrong. It seemed, at that moment, that nothing in my life could have been worse. But I kept laughing."

I came home and we had to rip out the carpet and deal with the insurance company to get it paid for. Just one more day in the life of the Nelsons.

A few days later, June 14, was my birthday. I was very depressed, but it had nothing to do with turning 29. If I'd stayed on schedule—the one I'd mapped out the day I took my first chemo—that would have been my last treatment. I was bummed out because of that. I should have been finished with all the crap, but I still had another month until my last treatment and another week of feeling lousy after that.

To make up for it, I decided to start letting my hair grow back. It had been coming in as my body got used to the chemicals. Now I'd let it come all the way in.

I was getting ready for life after wartime. My mom and dad came in for a visit at the end of June, and we went out to Main Street, a comedy club in Hackensack, New Jersey.

We sat in the back and tried to stay inconspicuous, but the guy on stage took one look at me, this huge guy with the stubby, nubby hair, and said, "You're either a state trooper, or a serial killer."

It was a funny line, and I could laugh. It was true, and it didn't bother me, because the end—the happy end—was near.

Chapter 16

It's Over

The cancer didn't kill me, but the stairs almost did.

I had started my last cycle. My hands and feet were getting worse every day, so Dr. Wolf decided not to give me any oncovin.

"Theoretically," he said, "you don't really need it, and I don't want to make your hands and feet any worse. So I'm not going to give you the oncovin."

"As long as you feel confident we don't need it..." I said. "If it's not essential, then don't."

I didn't want my hands and feet to get worse. They were non-functional at that point. I couldn't go for a walk with Brittany and Lyndsay. I couldn't do anything.

So Dr. Wolf just gave me the mustard and said, "Your hands and feet may get worse for another month, then should start getting better. Theoretically."

Theoretically took six months before they even started to get better and I still feel the effects today.

I was glad he stopped when he did. I wanted to kill the cancer, but I wanted to be able to walk again. Three days after that last MOPP, my legs were cramping up as bad as ever, and I felt it was working its way up through my body.

Not that my body was perfect anyway. Over the Fourth of July holiday, I was putting up a wallpaper border in Lyndsay's room, and I needed to hold it over my head and move it back and forth. My shoulder was grinding so loudly it was actually grossing me out. In that moment, I knew that even if the cancer hadn't come back, I couldn't have played again. That was when I admitted my shoulder was shot and that I wasn't ever going to come back.

On July 7, I got my last ABV. Dr. Wolf had gone on vacation, so I took it from Dr. Israel at his office across the street from Pascack Valley.

I went into his office and he said, "Okay, we'll hydrate you first, set up an IV, and give you a slow drip."

"What are you talking about?" I said. "That's not how I get it."

"Well," he countered, "what are you talking about?"

"Dr. Wolf just hooks up to the Broviac and shoots it in," I said.

I had to talk Dr. Israel into doing it my way. It's like he was a slow-drip man and I was a fuel-injection guy.

It was just another day, really. I didn't do any celebrating. It's hard to party when they've just pumped your body full of poison, even if it is for the last time.

It was rather uneventful. There were no big drum rolls or anything. I just talked Dr. Israel into doing it my way, and then I went home. I knew I still had to go through the rest of the cycle.

On July 13, I took my last prednisone and I was officially done. All I had to do was get the Broviac taken out and it was completely over, see you later.

I was finished with chemo, but the side effects were still with me and were going to be for a while, so I wasn't too excited. I cleaned all the pills out of our medicine cabinet, all the prednisone and procarbazine.

On Day 15, I knew my count would drop. I didn't know the stairs would almost kill me.

I've heard stories about vets in Vietnam who were in the last days of their tour. They'd refuse orders to do anything dangerous. They weren't going to get killed when they were so close to making it home.

I should have been like one of those short-timers, not taking any chances. But not me, not Karl Nelson. I was out there waving a red flag, shouting here I am, come and get me!

Bruno was back to paint the house. And I just had to help. It was July 15, a Saturday and Day 16 of my last cycle. My count was dropping, but that didn't stop me.

We had three storm doors that needed painting, and the glass was downstairs in our basement storage area. I decided to be a hero and carry them up to the garage for Bruno.

Normally, they wouldn't have been too heavy for me. And I got caught in an ego thing. I thought, I can still do that.

I picked up all three panes at once and came up the steps with them. By the time I got to the top, I was pretty wiped out. I should have taken a break then, but I didn't, because I'm stupid and I wasn't going to let anything like cancer slow me down.

My calves and feet were killing me, but I walked through our family room, through the kitchen and out the side door. I opened the screen door, took my second step out, and my foot didn't land flat.

But I couldn't feel it. I was just putting it out there again and hoping. This time, it landed on the side and it rolled.

I started to fall. I realized I didn't want the glass to break and have me fall on top of it, so as I was falling I threw it as far as I could, and it landed in a bush. Somehow, all three panes of glass survived without a mark.

I couldn't say the same for myself. I sat there for a few minutes, checking to make sure I hadn't broken any bones and adding up the damage: scrapes and bruises on both knees, scrapes on my shins, and cuts and bruises on my arm.

This was a bad time to get cuts, with my white count down. And especially outside, because who knows what's out there.

I was pretty rattled. But Heidi cleaned me up and took me back inside.

It was late in the morning, so I sat down to have some lunch. I was supposed to watch Lyndsay and relax, while Bruno went about his business, and Heidi and her brother were doing some work repairing the flood damage in the basement.

I was in the kitchen eating when something made me look over for Lyndsay. I just had a feeling. And when I turned, she was in her walker, right at the top of the stairs to the basement. Somebody had gone down and left the door open.

She was facing to go down and I just yelled, "Lyndsay! No!"

I got up as quickly as I could and tried to run from the kitchen, across the family room to the steps. But Lyndsay started going down. Suddenly, everything was in slow motion.

She went down, walker and all. I ran over, but my feet were so bad that I fell twice, catching them on the carpet and banging into the furniture. I got to the top of the stairs and took the fastest way possible, which was to slide down on my knees.

The stairs were plain wood, with no carpet or padding, but I threw myself down. I was scared to death something had happened to Lyndsay. I was terrified, but not about me. I didn't care if I got hurt. I just had to get down there for her.

Being an athlete, and then being a cancer patient, I tended to be a self-centered person. This was the first time Heidi ever saw me totally disregard myself for someone else.

I tumbled down the stairs, only to find that Heidi and her brother had already gotten to Lyndsay and, incredibly, she was fine. She had been flipped out of the walker, hit the wooden stairs, and landed on concrete. She ended up with a bump on her head and a black eye, but she was more stunned than hurt.

Meanwhile, I looked like hell with my knees all ripped up again. Heidi didn't know what to do, who to grab first, her baby or her husband.

"I saw the walker bound down the stairs and the baby bounce," Heidi said. "Then you came down right after her. I didn't know if you were dead, or if she was. I got the baby in my arms and checked her over. Then I took her upstairs and held her for a long, long time."

Bruno couldn't take it. He was a nervous wreck. There was no way he was getting back up on a ladder to paint the second story after watching those two accidents.

"That's it," he said. "I'm calling it a day. I'm bad luck here."

But he came back the next day and finished the job.

That was just a crazy, crazy day. That night, my hands were so tired I couldn't hold a fork tight enough to jab a piece of lettuce.

The next day, it was cold and damp and nasty outside. There was a drizzle and the temperature was in the low 60s. All day long, I had chills, but I thought it was just the lousy weather.

I never even thought about my count dropping, I don't know why. The first cycle, when I hit Day 15, I'd walked around with a digital thermometer in my mouth, and I drove Heidi crazy with it beeping every time I got a reading. This time, I didn't even think about it. But at about 10:30 p.m., I figured maybe I should check my temperature.

It was 101.1 degrees.

I didn't tell Heidi yet. We were upstairs in bed and I told her I was going down to read for a while. Once I got downstairs, I waited a few minutes and took it again.

It was 101.5.

I had to tell her now, and she wanted to kill me. She had me take some Tylenol and took my temperature again.

It was 101.7.

I was supposed to head for the hospital at 100.5, so I was already overdue, and the numbers were going in the wrong direction. At 11:30 p.m., I drove myself to the hospital, because there wasn't anyone to watch Brittany and Lyndsay. If we'd tried to get them up and dressed and into the car, it might have been too late.

I drove slowly and carefully, and once I got there, I got my IV right away.

My white count was down to 200, incredibly low. They did a blood test and found an infection in my system. It turned out it was from the Broviac, from where it entered under the skin. As careful as I'd been cleaning it, it had gotten infected. That's a drawback with that system. It's great for getting the drugs, but if you get an infection while you're getting chemo, it can kill you.

With the infection, I got really bad chills. I was lying in my hospital bed with six blankets piled on and I was still shaking. I just couldn't get warm.

The next day was Monday, July 17. They decided to take the Broviac out and that was fine with me. They hadn't planned to take it out until I'd had another CAT scan and some other tests that would prove I was perfectly clean. But in my mind, once they took that Broviac out, that was it. I was finished.

I figured it had been a surgical procedure to put it in, so it would be a surgical procedure to take it out. The doctor taking care of me that day told me he could do it right in the room and that it would take about 15 minutes.

Well, when they put my Broviac in, they must have done one great job, because it took this guy 45 minutes of digging to take it out. I was in the suite at Pascack Valley, under local anesthetic, trying not to watch him pulling and digging and pulling.

"It should be easier than this," he said.

Sweat broke out on his forehead. I started to wonder if he was nervous, or something was wrong. It was taking too long, and I could feel a dead kind of pulling in my chest.

When they had put the catheter in, they had placed a piece of cloth around the tubing to stop germs from traveling down the outside of the lines and into my body. The cloth is supposed to lie just below the skin, and can be pulled out from where the tubing enters the chest. Mine must have been buried deeper, because this doctor had a hard time reaching it. Finally, he had to cut around the collarbone to get it out.

That procedure left a big hole, 3/4 inch deep, 1/2 inch wide and 3/4 inch long. It looked like an ugly, open, empty eye socket. And he explained to me that he couldn't sew it up, because that was just begging for another infection, and my body couldn't handle it.

All they could do was pack it up, and change the packing every day, using a little less as it healed its way out.

It was pretty ugly, and it took three or four months to completely heal, but I was happy.

That's when I said, "I'm done. The damn thing is out and they're not going to put any more crap in me. No more pills. None of it. It's done."

I was a little upset with the way it had been done, but I was happy the catheter was out. I was drained, though, and I was still running a fever.

Without the Broviac, I had to take the antibiotics through an IV drip tube, and they were having problems with the veins in my hand. Eventually, the fever broke and I left the hospital.

That was July 22, 1989.

I had a CAT scan on July 28 and it showed up clean. Dr. Wolf was very happy with it. He told me he wanted to see me once a month, which is probably more than he needed to, but I wasn't going to argue. I figured he just must like me.

And it was over.

I'd beaten cancer. I'd beaten chemo.

I'd even beaten those damn stairs and lived to talk about it.

Chapter 17
Aftereffects

The next day of the rest of my life started out at the Giants' camp in Madison, New Jersey.

I got out of the hospital on July 22 and that Wednesday I was down at FDU-Madison, coaching the offensive line.

Let's make that "helping to coach" the offensive line. Fred Hoaglin was in charge. I was just there because the Giants had asked me to be there.

Bill knew I could only manage one practice a day. I even told him I wanted to use one of those folding seats that the old scouts sit on during practices.

"You can do that, Karl," he said, "but the guys will tease the hell out of you."

"Bill," I said, "I've put up with you all these years. They can't be any worse."

The most embarrassing thing was, I broke a couple of those seats. But the guys saw I could barely walk, so nobody hassled me.

I'd skip the morning practice and show up at 2:30. After practice, I'd stay for dinner and the night meetings, then drive home.

Coaching was a challenge, more with some guys than others. Like Brian Williams. He was the Giants' first-round draft pick in '89 and he wouldn't listen to anybody. He always knew more than anybody else. I'd tell him, "If you make a mistake and don't learn from it, you've made two mistakes."

Eric Moore was another one. He was another first-rounder in '88, one of the insurance picks the Giants made in case I couldn't make it back. I tried teaching Eric the same "heads-up" lesson that Tom Bresnahan had taught me back when I was a rookie, but he just wouldn't do it. Then, after two weeks of my constantly reminding him, he tried it my way and came over to me after practice and said, "You know what? That really works."

Overall, I enjoyed it. But George Young said I was too well-adjusted to coach and I think he was right.

During practices, my feet were still killing me. I was really worried about hitting a hole, falling down, and looking bad. I mean, I didn't look great at that point anyway, but I surely didn't want to trip.

Once, the lineman had to move from one drill to another all the way across the field. I could have gone around, but the quickest way was right up the middle of the field, right where the offense was setting up. I was going as fast as I could, but I just barely made it out of the way before the drill started. I don't know what Parcells would have said if I'd held up his little timetable. Probably just "Oops!" as they were scraping me off the field.

My feet hurt so bad I was doing anything to stay off them. I used the folding stools, or I'd drop to one knee. The pain was killing me, but I'd made a commitment to be out there, so I was out there.

I had a lot of pain in my legs, including some bad tendinitis where the Achilles tendon attaches at the heel. I was walking funny, when I was walking at all.

The cure? Ice, of course. I iced it every day after practice. Bill even let me. I guess if you melted down all the tons of ice I'd used for whatever reason over the years, it would be bigger than Lake Michigan.

On August 7, the team went up to New England for a week of practice against the Patriots. I debated going until I thought to myself, What are you, stupid?

At our camp in New Jersey, I had a car and they'd let me drive right up to the field so I could minimize the walking. Up in New England, I wouldn't have a car. I'd have to walk everywhere. And I'd be up there for two practices when I could really only make it to one, so I'd be sitting in my room doing nothing for a good part of the day. It didn't make a lot of sense. I told Bill, and he agreed.

I flew up at the end of the week to work the game for WNEW Radio. August 13, the day after I got back, I had a gallium scan. Dr. Wolf said the results were "fantastic." For him to use a word like that made me feel pretty good.

But I was still feeling the effects. My hair was growing back, but not my mustache. About this time, I had to go in for a photo shoot for one of the posters Tomorrow's Children was putting out. I'd been putting it off, but everybody else had gotten it done, so I had to take my turn.

The posters came out great, a series of 14 black-and-white portraits by Jerry Pinkus, one of the photographers who does a lot of work for the Giants. They look great, and I've got them all down in my basement in a big frame I made by hand.

There's Harry Carson, with his bag packed, heading into retirement; Bart Oates, the center with a law degree, holding his law books; Lawrence Taylor's got his golf clubs. Mark Bavaro, well, his mouth is shut, so it's perfect for him.

I didn't want mine taken, because I didn't have my mustache back. And I feel funny about how I look without my mustache.

My goal was to start growing it back in training camp, but it didn't work. It looked like a 12-year-old kid's mustache. In fact, it looked just like Jeff Hostetler's mustache.

I'm too proud of my mustache to let that happen, so I shaved it off again. And they took the picture without it. But the photo session had a happy ending.

David Jurist, the president of Tomorrow's Children, owns a printing company. Through a little computer wizardry, he took the mustache off another picture of me and stuck it on my portrait. And he did a great job. Unless you look really closely, you can't tell it's a fake.

My mustache caused me a lot of grief with Parcells. He always needed something to rag me about, just to let me know he still loved me. That's just the way he is.

I started growing my mustache back, officially and finally, on September 3. That was the day after the Giants' final preseason game.

It wasn't a real mustache for a month. The hair was peach fuzz, but it was still hair. Parcells called me a disgrace to the Giants organization because I was growing this scraggly mustache. He wanted to know if my mother knew I was growing it.

Well, my mom was here visiting us. I got her to write a note:

"Dear Bill: I want my son to grow his mustache back. I think he looks a lot better with it. Signed, Karl's Mom."

That shut him up.

Then he started needling me about all the awards I was getting again. I guess now that I was cured, he could treat me like that. Things were back to normal.

The Giants' first regular season game of the 1989 season was another Monday night against Washington, only this time it was at RFK. It had been a year since I'd made my comeback, but it seemed like a lifetime. And it nearly was.

What a difference. In '88, I ran out to a standing ovation. In '89, I had to climb up 30 rows of steep stairs to the top of RFK. That's where the broadcast booth is for the visiting radio team. My feet hurt and my legs were cramping so badly I had to stop twice. But I made it.

I was glad I was doing the game up in the booth. When I'm on radio, I have to stay controlled and I don't have time to get too emotional. I couldn't allow myself to have the normal reactions of a player who can't play and has to stay on the sidelines. I was very, very close to the team, still, but on radio I had to stay detached. That made it easier for me.

I was moving on through the aftereffects. Heidi was, too. Her aftereffects, not mine.

Heidi had been strong all the way through the treatments, but when they were done and she didn't have to be strong anymore, she crashed.

"I had a nervous breakdown and no one allowed me to have it," she says now. "That's typical. Most caregivers are strong the whole way through, but the minute they know that the other person is all right, they have emotional breakdowns.

"Karl was very self-centered, and that's the way it had to be while he was going through the treatments. He was number one in our house.

"While he was taking the treatments, I was like the grim reaper, always telling people bad news. When he went into remission, I didn't know what to say to people. Life was supposed to go back to normal, but I didn't know what normal was. It took me almost three years.

"I guess I didn't really believe it was over until Karl went for a three-year checkup and Dr. Wolf wrote me a letter after he got those results. That's when I finally knew it was behind us."

Her road to recovery was a long process. As soon as she knew I wasn't sick anymore, she realized that she could stop being the strong one, and her body finally gave in to her emotions. She'd wake up sick and have massive headaches and stomachaches the whole day. She was depressed and some days she just didn't want to get up off the couch. She didn't want to go anywhere or see anybody.

She tried to hide it for a while, but I could tell she wasn't well. I was doing what I could, but I couldn't help much. The shoe was on the other foot.

"The more people I talked to," Heidi says, "parents and other relatives of cancer victims, the more I learned that they all go through the same thing. That's why people say the patient goes through the treatments, but the family goes through the disease."

And they have their own aftereffects.

Heidi was running down. I tried to focus on her, but I'm not good at it. I tried to get some of the tension out of her life, but there wasn't much I could do. She was right in the middle of planning a big charity event, a fashion show and auction at the Short Hills Mall, and she was doing it all.

We finally relieved some of the pressure on a trip to San Diego. The Giants had a game there October 22, which just happened to coincide with the Leukemia Society of America dinner, where I was scheduled to get another award.

It was a great trip. We went out on Thursday and were able to relax completely, even though there was a Federal Express package with some final details for Heidi's fashion show waiting for us when we checked in.

We really got to enjoy San Diego. We walked around and did the San Diego Zoo, a great place, on Saturday. Then we went to the awards dinner that night. We just fell in love with the place. We'd move out there in a minute.

The trip to San Diego was a nice perk. I was still a little famous as the football player with cancer. That Thanksgiving, I was everybody's story again. HBO came to our house and filmed a segment for "Inside the NFL." CBS sent a camera crew to football practice one day to follow me around, and I caught a lot of grief for that from the players. They'd run up while the cameras were rolling and ask, "Coach Nelson, what's the snap count? Coach Nelson, who do I block on this play?" Of course, Parcells took all this in stride. Yeah, right.

During the games, the TV cameras would focus on me in the radio booth and the announcers would always point out that I was the guy with cancer. It was a little piece of what being Phil Simms or Lawrence Taylor must be like. People were asking for my autograph everywhere I went, and I had no privacy at all. At times, such attention can be great, though.

On December 2, I was honored as the Tomorrows Children's Fund Sportsman of the Year. Next to my comeback against Washington in the Monday Night game in '88, this award was Heidi's proudest moment.

Without the support of David Jurist, co-president of

Tomorrow's Children, I don't know how Heidi would have made it through my treatments. He became Heidi's best friend and confidant. So the award was personal, because we had done so much work and had given and received so much love from the group.

This is the charity that's closest to us, and 700 people were honoring me at a black-tie dinner at the Grand Hyatt in New York. Even though George Martin is the honorary president of Tomorrow's Children, we've got special ties to so many great people there because of what we've been through.

It was a great night. My parents flew in for the ceremony. Heidi wore a dazzling gold-lamé dress, and I had a gold bow tie to match her. George gave me an incredible introduction the way he always does, and when he did, I looked over at my dad. He had a tear in his eye. That was a special moment for me.

That's another trophy I keep right upstairs in the family room where everybody can see it. It's just beautiful and the inscription on it says:

"A shining star in times of darkness. For the gift of love that you have given to Tomorrow's Children."

In my speech, I thanked everybody and tried to say as much as I could about the kids, how they helped us and how much I learned from them. I wanted people to realize that, while we were having a great time, the reason we were there was because of the kids.

We stayed at the Hyatt that night and went to Giants Stadium for the game the next day. We were playing the Philadelphia Eagles and it was 25 degrees with a windchill factor near zero when I was out in the parking lot doing our "Tailgate Show."

When I got inside, I followed the first rule of broadcasting and went to the bathroom. But my hands were still numb from the chemo, and now they were frozen. I couldn't unzip my pants. And I wasn't about to ask anyone for help.

I finally got the zipper down, using both hands. Then it took another 10 minutes to get it back up.

That was just one of the problems I was still having. In October of '89, my feet still felt like two blocks of wood. I tried to run a lap on our grass practice field and I couldn't make the turns. Dr. Wolf said it would take about a month to get over, and it had been longer.

My feet weren't getting better. My whole body was much more sensitive to cold. When I went to school in Iowa, we had nine straight days when the temperature didn't get above zero, and it didn't bother me. But now the cold was just ripping through me. It killed my hands. I kept dropping the soap in the shower down at Giants Stadium, and, again, I wasn't about to ask anybody for help.

It took me until December before I could make one lap around the field. A week later, I officially retired.

It was toward the end of the season and I thought I might get some type of recognition from the Giants or the players. But I didn't get anything. That bothers me a little bit. When I was playing, every time somebody retired, somebody would collect 50 bucks from each team member to buy him a watch. I may not have played 10 years, but I was with the organization for seven.

George and Harry had retired the year before, and they were the guys who made sure things were taken care of. Gary Reasons, the team's new player rep, just didn't. Another reason may have been that most of the guys I had played with were gone. Brad Benson had retired, Chris Godfrey was gone, Billy Ard was playing in Green Bay. The team had changed over in two years.

I announced my retirement at the team's weekly press luncheon. I got to thank the Maras and the Giants. I acknowledged that they'd done anything I'd ever asked and had really taken care of me. And I thanked the press for getting out the message that people can survive cancer and go on to live successful lives.

I was happy I could make the announcement that I was leaving. Heidi always told me if you're a big enough man to play the game, be a big enough man to know when to leave. It would have been great to play another year or two but, even if I hadn't gotten the cancer, my shoulder was still bad.

I was fired up. Christmas was coming. The year before, Christmas just wasn't Christmas. But Brittany was old enough now to really get into it and Lyndsay was nearly a year old, a real little fireball.

Heidi was going to make sure our Christmas party made up for the disaster in '88 when I'd had that CAT scan and showed up late, with the bucket of chicken and the bad news that the cancer was back.

What felt a little weird was that I had had an MRI done Tuesday and the party had been scheduled for Friday. But this time, the test was clean, and we had the Christmas party December 22.

At least I thought it was a Christmas party. Everybody came in and handed me a gift, but I just put them by the tree. They were Christmas gifts, right?

Then, about half an hour into the party, Trish LaRose, one of our friends, handed me a gift and made me open it. It was a framed invitation to the party. And I didn't get what it was until I read, "Our holiday party is really a surprise retirement party... "

Heidi really got me. I had no idea. She had made me write out all the invitations to the party and then, two days later, sent out the second invitations telling everyone about the surprise.

It was a great night. Heidi had framed my Super Bowl jersey and they gave that to me. There were about 130 people there and it was just tremendous.

The Giants finished their regular season two days later, then lost in the first round of the playoffs in overtime to the Rams.

In January, I went back and did the Jimmy DiGisi basketball game and I apologized to the people. I told them, "The last time I was here, I couldn't be totally honest with you. I told you I beat cancer once. But I couldn't tell you it was back again. I apologize, but I've finished up my treatments and I'm proof they're doing great things. I feel confident they got everything this time."

I got a standing ovation.

A few weeks later, we did the Thurman Munson Memorial dinner. There was an ex-player there, a real legend in New York sports. He came up to me and said, "You know, you've been the subject of a lot of discussion at our house lately." It turned out his daughter had Hodgkin's.

I can't tell you who it was. His daughter's cancer was never made public, and I have to respect that. I remember I once got a call from Tomorrow's Children about a girl who was very upset because a newspaper had published a story about her without her knowledge or permission. She was devastated because it had been her decision to keep her story private. None of her friends knew she had it. I was asked to call her and try to cheer her up. It was one of the tougher calls I've made.

Each person has to deal with their situation on their own terms. Unfortunately, she didn't have that choice. It was taken out of her hands. I just told her about my decision to be open, and how the people who loved me and cared about me didn't let my illness affect them.

But it's usually a very private battle. Even public figures don't have to announce it to the press. Arthur Ashe tried to keep his fight with AIDS quiet until he was forced to admit it because of a newspaper investigation. That shouldn't have been their choice, it should have been his.

I thought about that at the Munson dinner. And I thought about something else. For the first time, I thought about what might have happened if I hadn't made it.

At the dinner, they did a flashback tribute to Munson, the catcher and captain of the Yankees' World Series winners in 1977 and '78, who died in a plane crash in '79. While they were showing it, I started thinking about his children growing up without a father.

I started thinking about what kind of things would be going on if I had died. Would Heidi be doing a dinner like this one about me? Yeah, probably. We knew enough people on the charity circuit that there would be something.

That's the first time I had thought about it. I always knew there were no guarantees. All I had to do was think about Colleen Radigan to know that.

Colleen was the receptionist at Giants Stadium. She'd had three bouts with cancer and when I was going through my treatments, she was going through some tough times herself. Whenever I was at the stadium, I'd make sure to stop by and we'd compare notes.

Colleen's cancer kept coming back and coming back. About a month before the season ended she was told she was clean after the third time through. Then, all of a sudden, it was back for a fourth time, and very quickly.

You could just tell she wasn't prepared to fight it. It's something you've got to be mentally ready for. She wasn't, and she went very quickly. She died right after the Giants lost the playoff game against the Rams.

It just shows what can happen when you don't have the fight in you, how quickly you can go. But I don't blame her. She put up the good fight three times and the cancer still came back. She just wasn't ready.

Hodgkin's disease is supposed to have a 90 percent cure rate, and mine came back. That's why I was a little more scared the second time.

There are no guarantees. All you can do is take it one day at a time, and hope they add up to a long and happy life.

Chapter 18
Friends and Family

In January 1990, "thirtysomething" was running its series of episodes on Nancy's battle with ovarian cancer.

We didn't really want to, but we ended up watching. They were very powerful shows. Some of the things were treated with a great deal of artistic license, but the way they showed people treating you when you have cancer was accurate.

People treat you differently when you have cancer. They try not to, but they do. Some people draw back. Others try to be overly nice, and you can tell the ones who aren't sincere from your true friends.

We had a lot of true friends. So far, we've given you our story. But part of the story is theirs. So we invited them to our house in Montvale, New Jersey in January of '93 to tell it.

We rounded up the usual suspects in our basement (the "Karl Nelson Hall of Fame"). I have all my football memorabilia up on the walls, pictures of me everywhere. Heidi always says that if something ever happened to her, our Brittany and Lyndsay wouldn't remember what their mother looked like.

It was January 13. We'd planned the get-together for a week, but the night before, Mario Lemieux, the superstar hockey player for the two-time Stanley Cup champion Pittsburgh Penguins, had announced he had Hodgkin's. It was a weird coincidence.

Matt Chambers, 35, is an accountant. I met him in 1983, the year I spent on Injured Reserve. Matt is precise, accurate, cautious—a perfectionist. He's very accommodating, very generous, just a sweet, gentle creature. He wants to make everybody happy, and he always puts that ahead of himself.

"I was thinking about Karl and getting together tonight,"

Matt said, "and then I heard him on the news, talking about Mario Lemieux. It was strange. I thought about when Karl was down at the Jersey Shore and he said his shoulder was bothering him. It was his last free weekend before the Giants started playing preseason games.

"The first time he had cancer, Karl was very calm. It must be that Midwest influence. You never see New Yorkers that way. He was so positive the first time through, you wouldn't have thought he had anything wrong with him. You'd just never have known this guy was sick.

"Karl was never much on talking about football with us. When we first met, he'd meet people and tell them he was an engineer. That was the year he was on Injured Reserve and didn't play. I guess he always seemed more like a guy who played football than a football player, if you see the difference.

"During his comeback, we went to see the San Francisco game, the one where he got hurt. Later that year, before the Jets game, we were out together and he said, 'I can't believe it. I think it's coming back.' I thought, He's such a nice guy. How can this happen?

"Karl was a professional athlete and I think they're different to begin with. They have different expectations. But I was amazed that he still tried to work out, even during the chemo. He never quit. That was incredible to me. I was amazed that things weren't going to faze him. He'd still want to go out and we'd make plans. Then he'd give us a call from the hospital and he'd be apologizing for canceling. I'd say, 'Karl! You're sick! Stop apologizing!'

"We did go out a lot, but we didn't talk about his cancer. It wasn't dinner conversation.

"Do I have any second thoughts about how we might have helped? The story's got a happy ending, so I'd have to say no."

Ellen Schmitz Chambers, 37, is Matt's wife. She just became the president of Creative Displays, and they're moving to Chicago. Matt met Ellen down at the Jersey Shore. She's on the ball, but off the wall. She's as professional as can be in her career, but with us she's a little kooky. (That's Heidi's word.)

"The only time I can remember Karl asking for anything special was at our wedding rehearsal," Ellen said. "When we were taking our vows, all the men were going to stand and he just said, 'I think I'm going to have to sit down.' So we had everybody sit down. That was in May of 1989, when his feet were really bothering him from the chemo.

"When we asked him to be in the wedding, he called us and wanted to know if we wanted him to be in the pictures, too. He had shaved off his hair and was wearing the hairpiece. And his color was awful. We said it was part of the deal, that he had to do it. We told him he looked great. Of course, he looked terrible."

Jay Ferriera, 35, is a landscape architect. I met him at Finnegan's through Rich Umphrey, who was the Giants' center when I spent my rookie season on Injured Reserve. His best friend lived next to Umphrey and we met and hit it off. When the Giants were on the road, I'd be at his place watching the games on television. He's a shrewd businessman and we've been friends for a long time.

"I went in for the chemo treatments with him," Jay said. "The limo would come and get me, then we'd pick up Karl. On the way into the city, I'd try to pick out the sights and all the stupid things you see going on, make fun of them just to pass the time so he wouldn't think about it. I never felt he dreaded it. It was just like when you'd see him after the game, with ice packs all over him. It was part of his way and you didn't question it.

"The first time he got the chemo, we were siting there in the doctor's office and we didn't know what to expect. The nurse came in with a pile of test tubes, and the doctor shot them in. I remember when the doctor told him he'd taste mustard, neither of us believed it, but he did.

"I was a little worried the first time we were in for chemo. We were talking about it and learned that it was all experimental dosages. They didn't really know what to do with a person his size. That bothered me. But it was a plus for me to build up the doctors. It helped put him more at ease.

"They've told Mario Lemieux that he has nothing to worry about, but that's what they told Karl the first time. The second time, he'd just gone through the radiation to get rid of it and it came back. I remember standing outside on a balcony at New York Hospital, looking at the boats in the East River. And he said, 'I have it again, and I've just got to deal with it.' He wanted to know what we had to do to get rid of it. He was still very calm, but the second time he knew it was really serious. It wasn't a quick thing. He wanted to take care of it and forget about football for right now. He was always asking the doctors

questions about his blood counts. The second time, he really
wanted to know what was going on.

"The mustache? That was one of his major concerns. I think
he worried more about losing the mustache than going bald.
He went to a guy on Route 4 to get the toupee, but he didn't
care. Heidi wanted him to wear it.

"A lot of times we knew what was going on with Karl, but
we couldn't say anything. Everyone knew we were close with
them, and they'd try to juice us for information. We couldn't
say anything, but didn't want to lie to them. To this day,
people still ask. I just did some landscaping for a synagogue
and the rabbi came out and asked, 'How's Karl Nelson?'

"I'd tell them he's fine. But I'd see him after the chemo, or
when he was quarantined in Pascack Valley. It showed that no
matter how big you are, it's going to knock you down.

"My advice to anyone with a friend going through it? Just
be there for them."

Dorothy Ferriera, 31, is a dental hygienist. I met her at one
of Jay's Halloween parties. She and Jay have two kids: Kyle, 5,
and Shelby, 1.

"When it first happened," Dorothy said, "I didn't know if
Heidi was going to be able to handle it. I was amazed at how
good she was.

"Heidi showed it more. Karl was quiet. He was too quiet. I
was worried about it. He didn't talk a lot about it. You don't
want to push it, but this is a major thing. It's not like a cold.
He was so stoic, I just worried about what was going on inside.
But now I can say that that's just the way he is.

"Karl seemed more serious about it the second time. He
talked more about it, and it seemed like it hit him that it was
real. Before that, during the radiation, it was 'I'm Karl, I'm
fine, I always do well.' He had a lot of denial. When it came
back, he definitely was more serious about it.

"Heidi told me the cancer was back at the Christmas party
in '88. They'd found out earlier that day. I get upset now just
thinking about it. We were in the kitchen. I don't remember
the exact words. We had five minutes alone, then she had to
go back and be the hostess. I admired her for doing so well
with it. She was freaking out inside, but holding everything
together so that everybody would be fine at this party. She
didn't want to have to tell everybody. I remember having to
sit there and pretend things were normal and wonderful

when I'd rather have been home hysterical.

"When Lyndsay was born, Heidi had the fear that she was going to have to raise these two kids by herself. She had felt so safe after the first cancer that she went ahead and had the second child, and then she was petrified of being alone.

"I understood how she felt when Lyndsay was born, about wanting Karl to be healthy instead of having a new baby. I don't know if she said that in those words, but the feeling was clear to me, and there was nothing wrong with it.

"I didn't try to Pollyanna it, because I was scared, scared for him. Our next door neighbor had died of a lymphoma and I remember my neighbors saying, as he was dying, that it wasn't cancer that was killing him, it was drugs. I was just so afraid this time, more frightened than the first, because it was chemotherapy instead of radiation. But I hid it from them. I don't think I said how afraid I was.

"When I see pictures of him from that time, it amazes me how bloated his face was, and I didn't notice it at the time. It didn't hit me. Just a while ago, Lyndsay and I were looking through photo albums from that time, and she didn't recognize him. He really was so different. I don't remember him looking that strange.

"I remembered that they'd had problems with his size with the radiation, that the machine wasn't big enough for Karl. Part of me was angry at the doctors when it came back the second time. If they had known their stuff and had figured it out right the first time, they probably would have gotten it.

"My overall advice would be to go at the other person's pace. Don't push it too much. Get on the phone or go see them, ask how they're feeling, and then drop it. You have to show concern, because that's important too, but don't harp on it.

"It was the same with football. Karl would talk football all the time with people, but I think one of the things they liked about their friendship with us was that it wasn't a football friendship. We talked more about landscaping.

"He was somebody outside of football, and he was somebody outside of the illness, too. People get so focused on that, and they need to continue some normalcy.

"It's hard, but you just don't push it. Make sure they know there's an opening to talk if they want to, but don't harp on it. People who have to know every detail can be annoying."

Jay Goldberg, 33, is my agent, the one who came to the

hospital and hooked me up with WNEW Radio. I can't begin to tell you what lengths Jay will go to for me, or for any of his clients.

"I never remember Karl complaining," Jay said. "Not about anything. It was always like the time I went to see him in training camp, when he was making the comeback. He was walking across the field with Heidi, towards me. And he had ice strapped to his shoulder, and to his knees and to his ankles. He was covered with it. I asked him, 'How do you feel?' He just smiled and said, 'Great!'

"The only time I heard him complain was after the thoracotomy and the laparotomy, when he was in so much pain he had to ask the nurse for more painkillers. And I really wouldn't call that complaining."

Tricia LaRose was 16 when we met her as a busgirl at Finnegan's. She's 25 now, and we like to think we nurtured her and brought her along. Trish is still very innocent in a lot of ways. She's a good girl and she will drop her life to take care of her friends. She was right there for Heidi and me when the cancer first hit, taking care of the house and whatever we needed, and she's right there still.

"When I heard about Mario Lemieux, Karl was the first person I thought about. I remember when he first got it, he really took it in stride. He was really calm. The doctors made it seem to him that he had no problem, that he was going to be fine, and that he had nothing to worry about at all. That's what they're doing with Lemieux.

"The night they called Heidi and told her Karl had cancer, she came to my house and I drove with her to New York. She wouldn't let me drive. She had to be in charge. And she drove like a lunatic. But Karl was pretty calm about the whole thing, and I was surprised.

"I remember taking all those phone calls when it happened. I didn't know what to tell anybody. There were just rumors. Heidi told me who I could tell. But the phone rang non-stop. People were heartless; they didn't want to leave them alone. I did a lot of things around the house while Karl was in the hospital, food shopping and taking care of the dog. I stayed over every night. I was going into my sophomore year in college down in Florida, and I asked my parents if I could stay here. I didn't want to leave Heidi and Karl. They told me to get on with my life, but it was very hard on me. I had an article

from the newspaper with a picture of Karl, and I got it framed
and had it with me down at school.

"The second time, I remember Karl being aggravated that it
came back. He would get mad at it. Heidi's stomach started
bothering her then.

"With Heidi, you tried to hide your worries because it would
make her worse, she would worry about you worrying about her.

There was one other friend there that night. Billy Blanchard,
42, the manager of Finnegan's, who sat quietly on the couch
and never said a word.

We're always surprised when we invite him somewhere and
he actually shows up. He just doesn't like to leave Finnegan's.
But he takes care of his "family" there. And not just us, but all
the regulars who come down to his place in shifts.

You could tell he was uncomfortable that night. It just
wasn't his kind of setting. But a few days later, he came by
with a nine-page, handwritten letter. And this is some of it:

"The round-table format is not a venue I am particularly
good at...

"I first met Mr. Nelson in the spring after he was drafted.
Friendships grew, real friendships, and not jock-sniffing, pseudo
'I know so-and-so.' I never wanted the place to be a jock
hangout. Karl was a nice guy who happened to possess the
talent to play for the Giants.

"As a preface, my mother died of cancer at Sloan-Kettering
after five years of hope, despair, anger, confusion, hurt,
disillusionment, and intense family pain.

"Trish called me the day before the operation to say they
had found 'something,' a word that connotes the worst of
thoughts and feelings. I drove Heidi and Ms. LaRose to the
hospital the next day.

"When Karl was told, Heidi and I walked to the balcony
overlooking the river and talked. She was beginning to order
herself emotionally and brace herself for the challenge in front
of her. Ms. Nelson had all the right qualities to help her
husband: toughness, honesty, compassion. She was nice to me
and other inquirers, when 'Please, give us space' is a common
thought for cancer families.

"The courage and grace of both Karl and Heidi, the
willingness to face the greatest and most dangerous challenge
a young family could face, is a poignant example and inspiration
to many people. More people will benefit from knowing the

trials and tribulations of Mr. and Mrs. Nelson, than from any NFL career."

These people who have been our friends for nearly a decade were our support system. There were others, too, like Brett Korbel and Darren Rizzi, two kids from a local high school, whom we recruited to help us work around the house while I was undergoing treatments. And of course, our families, especially Heidi's mother, Jeanne Stegemann, and sister, Donna Hellstern, who took care of Brittany and Lyndsay and our house and us.

Friends and family.

We couldn't have done it without them.

Chapter 19
How to

You live and learn.

It's not always easy to know what to do when the doctor tells you that you have cancer.

Experience, unfortunately, is the only teacher. But you can take some advice from people who have been there before.

People like us.

We sat down and tried to come up with some practical advice for cancer patients, especially first-time cancer patients. Some of it is what we learned from people who passed it to us, things that worked. Some of it is what we learned by trial and error, things we found out later.

We made our own mistakes and tried not to make the same ones twice. Our basic plan is a four-step process: Confront, Challenge, Conquer, and Continue.

<u>Confront it</u>. The faster you learn to accept a situation, the faster you can be on the road to recovery. Once you can admit what you have, it's easier to deal with it. You have to face it head on, to be able to say "cancer."

<u>Challenge it</u>. You've got to see it as a fight, because that's what it is. And you've got to be willing to do whatever it takes to win that fight.

<u>Conquer it</u>. The battle itself is the next step. Use all the weapons at your disposal. It is, literally, life or death.

<u>Continue</u>. Once you've won, move on. Cancer may be the biggest thing that you will ever have to deal with. But when you've beaten it, you've got to move on with your life. Sometimes, that's the hardest step of all.

Cancer isn't hidden in a closet anymore, the way it was a few decades ago. We'd like to think that people like us, celebrities who have talked about their illnesses and their treatments openly, have made others more aware.

We've listed some practical advice—our "How To" guide, including big things and little details. We hope that what we've been through can help you or someone you know.

First, find a doctor you're comfortable with, one you trust.

Choosing your doctor is one of the most important things you will do. You'll probably get recommendations from the doctor who makes your diagnosis and from family and friends who have been through cancer treatment.

Remember that you don't have to take the first one who comes along. Look until you find a doctor who fits.

Doctors deal with hundreds of cases of cancer every day. They're used to dealing with it, but it's your first time, and you don't know what to do. You're going to do whatever they tell you to do, so it's very important that you get somebody you're comfortable with.

Interview several doctors, establish a relationship before your treatment begins. Doctors are the greatest salesmen in the world, because nobody ever questions what they say. The practice of medicine is not an exact science, however, and doctors don't know everything.

The first time through, I just trusted any doctor. The Giants found Dr. Wolf for me, and he set me up at Sloan-Kettering for my radiation treatment because he thought it was the best thing for me.

They were good doctors, but my size created some problems for them. If somebody else had treated me, would they have gotten it all the first time? I don't know.

I'm just damn glad I had Dr. Wolf, who is a chemotherapy specialist, the second time. He followed my radiation treatments, even though he wasn't in charge, and I trusted him.

Ask questions—not to find out if they know what they're talking about, but to see if you're comfortable with them. That comfort zone is the biggest thing. The doctor is going to put you through hell and you have to go through it with someone you trust. I tell people that if you believe what you're going through is helping you, it is. If you don't believe it's helping you, then it's not, and you're not going to make it. You must have absolute trust in your doctor so that there's no doubt in your mind that what he's doing is helping you.

Designate a "treatment coordinator."

You need somebody to order all your tests, and to collect

and coordinate the results. Often, you're bounced from doctor to doctor along the course of your treatment. The second one doesn't necessarily know what the first one has done, and hasn't seen the results of tests that might greatly change the course of treatment. Or the second one might order a test and not send the results back to the first.

The bottom line is that you might not get something you need, or you might get something you don't.

Treatment coordination doesn't really exist now. That's probably a new job field that will be developed in the next 10 years. (There is some advice for medical centers and hospitals.)

Until it becomes standard operating procedure, you've got to pick your own coordinator. Tell your doctor, "You're my man. I expect you to be in charge of everything. If you order a test, make sure everyone else gets the results. If you refer me to somebody else and they order a test, I want you to make sure you get the results, and then distribute it to whoever needs it."

If your doctor's not willing to do that, find another doctor.

I found out how important this was, firsthand. During the summer of 1988, when I was getting ready for my comeback from radiation treatments, I had a scheduled checkup with Dr. Wolf, and he found a problem with one of the protein levels in my blood. Sloan-Kettering had missed it, but Dr. Wolf found it.

It was a normal checkup. But at the time, I was bouncing back and forth between Sloan-Kettering and Dr. Wolf. I was seeing one of them every three months, which meant I was at each place just once every six months. That wasn't a smart thing to do.

If Sloan found the protein problem, they never reported it back to Dr. Wolf or did any further checks of their own. It wasn't a major problem, but it could have been. Every patient deserves their absolute attention. We were very upset with them about that, and it was the last time I went back to Sloan-Kettering for a checkup.

Try not to let that happen by naming a treatment coordinator. And make sure you check up on him, too. If you take a test somewhere else, make sure you ask your doctor if he's gotten the results. Know what tests you're taking and make sure all your doctors are aware of them. Don't assume they'll share the information. They should, but it's your responsibility to make sure they do.

Don't allow yourself to be treated like a number.

You're a person, an individual. You have individual needs. You need to be treated like a person, even if you're at someplace like Sloan-Kettering, where they're treating thousands of people. Keep your own identity.

You can do that by making sure the people treating you see you as a person. The radiation techs at Sloan were very friendly, and it wasn't because I was a football player. They were nice people. If you're open with them, they'll be open with you. Don't become just another body that's there to get radiated. If you give them a chance to ignore you, they will.

Be pleasant. Joke around. Ask questions. Do anything so you're not just walking in the room, lying down, getting treated, and walking out. If you do that, you will be just a number to them.

Establish the relationship early, so when you do have a down day (and you will) they'll be willing to help you through it. At some point, there's going to be a problem with your course of treatment, and you want these people on your side.

You may hate what they are doing to you, but don't hate the people. Treating cancer patients is a hard job. If you can help them to feel better about it, it will come back to you. They'll go out of their way to help you.

Remember, cancer is the enemy. And you're all individuals, fighting it together.

If you don't know, ask.

Ask every dumb question you can think of. And that's coming from the man who never asked any questions.

Too many people just do what they're told. You have the right to understand what's happening to you.

When they're talking about putting poison into your body and saving your life, no question is dumb. If your doctor gets tired of answering questions, find another doctor.

Keep a log of how you feel. It can help you find what's causing certain problems. Take the log with you when you visit your doctor. His time is valuable and so is yours. You don't want to waste it, and you don't want to forget anything. A log helps to keep you organized.

Get as much literature as possible and read it. Then, if you don't understand something, ask.

You don't want to become a doctor. You just want to know what's going on so that, if things don't seem right, you can recognize it.

Some doctors just don't tell you enough. During my early

chemo, my stomach felt as if it were being ripped apart. Then, the first time I wound up in the hospital with my white count dangerously low, we picked up some pamphlets about what the different drugs were and what the side effects were. There were some things about what to do and what not to do. As it turned out, I wasn't supposed to eat bananas because of the procarbazine. And I wasn't supposed to eat fresh fruit or yogurt because of the bacteria in them. I wouldn't have known any of that if I hadn't read the brochures. Nobody had told us.

The scariest things can be the ones you don't know about. If you want to find out, ask.

If possible, get a catheter.

If you're getting chemo and your doctor gives you the option, get a catheter. I had a Broviac. There are other types. There's less mental anguish with a catheter.

A catheter can help keep you on schedule during your cycles. With other means of treatment, the veins in your arms may break down. You don't want to miss a treatment because they can't find a vein.

A catheter also can keep the chemo from leaking out of your veins and onto your arms. When that happens, the chemo will eat away the skin, and that's one more problem you don't want to worry about.

You might be turned off by the idea. Fifteen inches of tubing coming out of your chest isn't very pretty. But you get used to it very, very quickly.

The downside of having a catheter is the chance of infection. That happened to me in my seventh cycle. And I've talked to people who have had two or three replaced. You just have to be very careful with it. Overall, the benefits outweigh that risk.

Keep a positive mental attitude.

We can't say enough about that. People have written books about healing your body with your mind.

Did I want to heal it with just my mind? No. I wanted to take advantage of everything the doctors could do to help me. But I knew that by staying positive, I was helping them to help me.

Some people believe in the effectiveness of imagining their white cells attacking the cancer cells. There have been cases in which doctors have stopped treatments and told people they were going to die, and the patients somehow made it through using the visualization method.

Trust science, but use a little faith.

Again, if you believe it's helping, it probably is. If you don't believe it's helping, it probably isn't.

If you're not a positive person, become one. If you're not going to do it for yourself, do it for your spouse or your kids or your friends. Find a reason to make it through.

Cancer can change your attitude. One of our engineers on WNEW's Giants broadcasts was the kind of hypochondriac who'd sneeze and take two days off from work. If you asked him how he was, he'd tell you. In detail. But he came down with cancer and changed completely. I never heard him complain again.

Remember, odds are for suckers. If they give you a 10 percent chance of beating it, you've got to believe you're in that 10 percent, or you'll end up in the 90 percent real quick.

Find inspiration wherever you can. Just look at Dennis Byrd, the New York Jets defensive end who was paralyzed in a game in 1992. They said he'd never walk again, but two months later, he left New York walking on crutches, and he was heading for further recovery.

The mind is a terrible thing to waste. Use yours as another weapon in your battle against cancer.

Find someone who's been through what you're going through and is still around to talk about it.

There are lots of support groups out there that will help you find someone who's had the same type of cancer you've got, and beaten it with the same type of treatment you'll get.

I was lucky that Jay Goldberg hooked me up with Jeff Blatnick, the Olympic gold medal winner. Jeff was an athlete who had had Hodgkin's and came back to compete on a world-class level.

There's strength in numbers. It's like training camp. If you had to go through it alone, you'd quit a lot quicker than if you have 40 or 50 guys to lean on and share your hard times.

There are support groups, led by a survivor and made up of current patients. They can really help. You can find them through your treatment center or through many charities. Tomorrow's Children, for instance, has a service to match up kids who have similar forms of cancer for support.

You've got to be careful, though. No two cases are exactly alike and that can make it dangerous to compare. Mario Lemieux' Stage I Hodgkin's, the most treatable form of cancer, is not the same as bone cancer or liver cancer.

Make sure everyone gets what they need.

There are support groups for cancer patients and for their families. I was offered counseling, but I didn't think I needed it, and I never thought to ask if Heidi needed counseling. It probably would have helped her, but she never knew it was available.

Find out what counseling is available, for yourself and your family. Then use it, if you're comfortable with it. Don't force it on anyone, including yourself, but keep an open mind. Talk to people. It could really help.

As for your friends, you've got to be the counselor. And for your employer, you have to be the educator. Let them know what you're going through and what they can expect. And let them know things might not go exactly according to plan.

The more they know about what you're going through, the more they can help you through it.

But don't feel obligated to talk to people about your cancer. It is a personal thing. If you don't feel like talking about it at that time or place or to that person, call a time out. When I was in Finnegan's and didn't want to talk football, Billy Blanchard, the bar manager, would always call me away for a phone call. Steer the conversation the way you want it to go, even if it finally means being blunt.

Cancer is the major thing happening in your life and people will want to discuss it with you, but there will be times you won't want to. That goes for your spouse, too.

Try to make people comfortable, but if they can't deal with it, stay away from them.

Don't play the martyr.

Don't try to stand on your own. Don't be too proud to ask for help when you need it. And don't feel guilty about asking for it, either.

You need the help, and the people around you need to help you. Remember, you're all in it together. It's not fair to say, "It's my battle, I'll do it all myself."

You're the one going through it, but you're not the only one experiencing it. It's frustrating for your family and friends when they don't know what to do to help you. You have to let them participate.

You have to pay attention to relationships. There are a lot of breakups and divorces when people go through treatment and right after it. Be aware of the stress you're putting on your relationships. Recognize that you're a different person during treatments.

Try to be yourself as much as possible.

Your lifestyle will change, but try to keep it normal. Stay in routines as much as you can. Try to keep yourself in position in life so that when you get back, you won't find the world has gone on without you. Don't use cancer as an excuse to drop out of life. Absence may make the heart grow fonder, but most times it's more like "out of sight, out of mind."

Ask for sleeping aids or tranquilizers if you need them. Sleep is important. So is feeling comfortable about yourself. You're already pumping chemicals into your body, causing a lot of adverse reactions. If you can take something to counteract the side effects–like the anxiety, depression, and wild mood swings from prednisone–do it. The more you feel like yourself, the happier you and everyone around you will be.

Plan something special for your "good" days. Even in chemo, you can plan your cycle to some degree. Take advantage of your good days. Have a picnic, go to the beach, ride bikes. There aren't many days you'll feel great, so make the most of the ones you get.

Tune your body and keep in tune with your body.

If you were working out before, try to continue working out, but don't expect to do what you could before. The better shape your body's in, the better the healthy cells will be able to fight off the effects of radiation or chemotherapy.

If you weren't working out, you can start. Don't run five miles a day, but try walking. It's a great way to relieve stress. Just remember to get your doctor's approval before doing any kind of exercise program.

When you're working out, listen to your body. If you're not sure you can do something, don't do it. If you push your body too far, it will get back at you. The only time I got sick during my radiation treatments, I didn't listen to my body. I hadn't gotten much sleep, and I went out and lifted heavy rocks and dirt. I got sick. It was my body saying, "You shouldn't have done that."

Exercise is important. So is rest. Schedule a time during the day to take a nap if you need one. Your body is being poisoned and you want to give the good cells the chance to survive by giving them enough rest.

Eat to live.

Keep your weight up. Eat, even if what you're eating is fattening. This is no time to worry about your figure.

Eat even if you can't taste it. It's part of your job, part of your treatment. Eat more on days when you feel better. There will be other days when you won't be able to.

Be careful, though, to check the handbooks and ask your doctor to find out what you should and shouldn't be eating.

And drink plenty of water. It will help to flush the toxins out of your system.

Look for the little things.

When I was taking the chemo, I started to have a gag reaction. Heidi noticed it and suggested I suck on a sourball while Dr. Wolf gave me the injection.

Simple, but it worked.

There are other little things that helped. When the chemo dried out my skin and made my back break out in acne, we found out that soybean massage oil was a cure. When my taste died, Heidi mixed up Bacardi mixers, with no alcohol and very little water added, to give me a little taste sensation.

Don't forget the little things that can help you get around the side effects. If there's a little thing that can make your treatment easier, do it.

Find little positives, and avoid little negatives. For me, the triggers were baking soda, exhaust fumes, and strawberry yogurt. Maybe it was physical, maybe it was psychological, triggering an association with my treatments. Either way, they made me sick to my stomach.

Do what you can to avoid the triggers. And tell your family and friends about them, so they can help you avoid them, too.

Money is not the object.

Cancer treatment is expensive, and not everyone is lucky enough to have an organization as good to them as the Giants were to me.

But worrying about the bills will complicate your treatments and add stress, something you don't need.

Work out a payment schedule with your doctors. Most will do that.

You can also get help from charities. There are lots of them out there, and some provide financial support for cancer patients. Talk to social workers, hospitals, or your religious group to find out more. Do the research. It can pay off.

Let your spouse help by handling the worry about the bills. That might sound unfair, but you'll be better off for it.

The most important thing is your recovery. You'll have time to worry about the bills when you're through it.

Don't forget your checkups.

When you're done with your course of treatment, make sure you go for all your checkups and tests. Don't be afraid that they'll find something wrong again. You can't stick your head in the sand. If there is a recurrence, the sooner you find out and start to beat it, the better off you'll be.

Then, once you've beaten it, get on with your life as soon as you can.

Chapter 20
Giving Something Back

Cancer wasn't a call to us to start giving something back. We started way before that.

In 1984, our life was really coming together. My football career was ready to take off and we felt blessed with our beautiful daughter Brittany and a beautiful house. We felt fortunate. And we wanted to share our blessings with people who needed our help.

We started working with the Lupus Foundation. Heidi got to know some people there when she modeled in a fashion show for them, and they asked me to be their celebrity spokesman in 1985. We were proud of that.

A lot of the players were lined up with charities. We just wanted one that could be our own.

The running backs and quarterbacks get asked by all the "big-name" charities, but a lineman is just happy to take what he gets. The Lupus people appreciated us, even though I wasn't a big-name player.

We did work for Lupus, but that didn't mean we did work only for them. Back then, when a guy would have an event for his charity, all the other guys would show up to help. That's how I first came in contact with Tomorrow's Children, George Martin's charity.

That was before I got cancer. We were giving back because we felt lucky. After I got cancer, we started giving back for other reasons.

Everybody tries to find a way to handle serious illness. Part of Heidi's answer was to throw herself into work with the Tomorrows Children's Fund. To her, the more money she raised for kids with cancer, the more she was helping her husband.

And because of what I was going through, she became their best asset.

"I was the wife who could go into stores and ask people to donate money to an ad journal," Heidi said. "People were very receptive to me."

Heidi's reaction was not unusual. A lot of people are drawn into charity work when a tragedy hits close to home. They want to do what they can to help, and for some of them, what they can do is volunteer their time or raise money for their cause.

There are a lot of charities out there, too, doing all kinds of work. There are charities for research, charities for treatment, charities for support, charities that provide financial aid. And there are some charities, big ones like the United Way and the American Cancer Society, that try to do it all.

We first had contact with Tomorrow's Children through George Martin. We went to a dinner honoring him as their "Sportsman of the Year," the award I'd get a few years later. We really got turned on by it, by the people there.

It wasn't just the money they raised to help children with cancer. It was the awareness they were bringing to these young victims that was almost as important.

With my Hodgkin's, the link with Tomorrow's Children naturally grew.

Heidi is really our driving force. She does 90 percent of the work, and I get 100 percent of the credit. I'm the one with the name, the one who gets to stand up and accept the plaques and awards. Sometimes that doesn't seem fair, especially when I think about how much she's done.

And she's done some great things. There was one fashion show at the Woodcliff Lake Hilton late in the '88 season when she raised over $27,000 on her ad journal, hitting up every little shop between here and Giants Stadium. I was so proud of her for that. And it couldn't have come at a better time. I was fighting through my ankle injury and I hadn't been looking forward to the show. But I got to start against New Orleans, the week before the show, and when I put on my tux and walked her, seven months' pregnant with Lyndsay, down the runway, I felt so good about what we'd done, together.

Heidi became the center of attention for a lot of the Tomorrow's Children efforts. After all, we were raising money for children with cancer and I had cancer. She was the obvious focal point for the media.

Where do you go when you want to help? That depends on what you want to do.

Sometimes, people who are helped by one charity's service turn around and give the same type of help to others. It may be driving patients to and from their chemo treatments, or leading support groups for patients and their families.

Other people are more comfortable just raising money. Whatever you do, it will be appreciated.

When you're sizing up a charity to work for, don't be afraid to ask why the people are involved. Look for a personal connection between the people and the work they do. We've found that smaller charities tend to give you more personal satisfaction. If you have any doubts about the charity, find another one. There are plenty of great organizations out there. Be comfortable.

We've told you about the good feeling we got from the people at Tomorrow's Children when we first had contact. My battle with cancer just made the link stronger.

Tomorrow's Children has changed, though, since we began our association with it. It's growing, getting larger. Tomorrow's Children now runs over 200 events, including some big-time fund-raisers.

Like all charities that have raised more and more money, Tomorrow's Children has come to rely on corporate donations, through events like the radiothon run by WFAN, New York's 24-hour sports radio station.

Those big donations may make the little work—the car washes, the bake sales, the raffles—seem less significant. But if the big money hurts the "grass roots" campaign, it misses the point. Because it's not just the money that is important, but also the awareness that's raised.

Every charity needs all the help it can get, and all the ways to raise money it can find. How many are there? Many. Auctions, dinners, dances, carnivals, softball games, golf outings, tennis outings, basketball games, swimming, running, walking, biking, baseball card shows, trick-or-treat drives, candy sales, fashion shows, celebrity posters, radiothons, corporate challenges, donated concerts or plays, ad journals... the list is absolutely endless, limited only by your imagination and energy.

We still do three or four events for the Lupus Foundation every year and we do anything Tomorrow's Children asks. We also try to help out other charities if we can, but there's only so much time available. If we wanted, we could do an event every night and that would be our full-time job.

Sometimes, you've got to draw the line. I don't have a

ballplayer's big salary. I've got to work hard just to make a living. But it's difficult to say no. If you don't do an event, people think you're turning your back on them. They don't realize how many events we're asked to do, and that we're trying to live our lives, too. One of the reasons I fought so hard was so I could be with my family. I need to spend time with them.

Charity work isn't something you have to do. It's something you have to want to do. And we enjoy doing our share.

Like most people who have been through a fight with cancer, we feel indebted. We pay back the debt the best way we can. Whatever you put back comes to you again.

When we were going through our own hard times, we drew tremendous support from the people around us, including the people at Tomorrow's Children. Some of the kids Heidi and I worked with were in worse shape than I was, but they always had a smile for us.

You can find worthwhile charities everywhere. Michael Gillick isn't with Tomorrow's Children. In fact, he and his mother are the co-founders of their own organization in Ocean County, New Jersey, called "Oceans of Love."

I met Michael one day when someone brought him to Giants Stadium. Michael has neuroblastoma, and he is terminal. This little boy, who has been ravaged by cancer from the day he was born, has been such a pillar of strength for me. When he was born, the doctors didn't give him two months to live. He's 14 years old now.

Michael's favorite phrase is, "When life gives you lemons, make lemonade." Things keep happening to him, but he keeps going.

He's an incredible little boy. He's had tumors that have put pressure on his optic nerves and have cut off his sight. He's had tumors in his back that have broken the bones in his spine. But he's always upbeat, always positive. I don't know how he does it, but I admire him for it.

We developed a real relationship. We talk each week to discuss the Giants' next opponent, and he tells me what the Giants should do and what to say to the players.

I have got a picture of Michael and myself taken when we were out in California at Super Bowl XXI. I had told him I had it taped right to my desk at home, but he didn't really believe me. Then, when *Sports Illustrated* ran a big feature on my comeback in 1988, they used a picture of me sitting at my desk at home. You could make out the snapshot of Michael and me in the background. He was so thrilled he called me right away. It felt so good to make him feel good.

Sometimes, I'll go a few weeks without talking to him, and then I'll be afraid to call him, afraid that there'll be bad news about him. But I always call and I always feel better after I do.

Of course, I can do some things as a celebrity that other people can't. And as someone who's been through cancer, I can relate to some of the things that the kids are going through.

During my treatments, I'd go down to see the kids from Tomorrow's Children, and I'd make sure I'd leave the hairpiece behind. I wanted them to see that I was just like them, that I was going through what they were going through. And that we were going to make it.

Today, I still do one-on-one calls with people who contact me when someone in their family gets Hodgkin's. I spend hours on the phone with these people. I can't talk to them all, but I do what I can.

We were lucky enough to have a good life before the cancer. And we were lucky enough to hang onto life through the cancer.

If that doesn't make you want to give something back, nothing will.

Chapter 21
Life Goes On

What do I want to be when I grow up?

Once cancer was behind me, all I had to do was figure out what I wanted to do with the rest of my life.

Late in the '89 season, I was getting frustrated. I had five jobs, but all of them were part-time. I was working at National Insurance Associates (NIA), coaching with the Giants, doing their games on radio, doing speaking engagements, and doing charity appearances. But there was nothing permanent, nothing fixed. Our life had no set schedule.

I wasn't dedicating myself 100 percent to anything. As a football player, you do the best you can. That's the way you're taught. But after football, I wasn't able to do that.

My life was in limbo—all wait-and-see: wait and see if I was in remission, wait and see if the cancer would come back. Everything seemed up in the air.

Some of it started to clear up in December when I retired from the Giants, which officially ended my link with the team.

Football is not real life, not by any means. I had to make an adjustment and it wasn't easy.

I have always said I'd planned on retiring from the day I started playing and that's helped a lot. But I still had to realize that I couldn't live the same lifestyle after I'd retired.

For instance, in 1989, we bought a new car, a Chevrolet Lumina. When you play for the Giants, you do a few commercials and you get a Cadillac or a Chevy Blazer for six months, free of charge. When you have to buy your own car, it's a different story.

I'm making decent money with NIA and my radio work, but we've got a big house. I'd planned on playing another three years, at least, and having the house paid off by the time I retired. It just didn't work out that way.

At NIA I work in the area of insurance and financial services, primarily in pensions. I specialize in 401(K)s, insurance for estate planning, life insurance, disability insurance, and health insurance.

Being Karl Nelson, ex-Giant, helps me get in the door. When I began working at NIA full time in February of '90, I wore my Super Bowl ring. Before that, I never wore it unless I was making an appearance. Now I wear it all the time. I don't take it off in public places, and I don't usually let people try it on. They can see it, but it stays on my finger. And if I do take it off, I joke that I'm staying between them and the door. I say it as a joke, but that's exactly what I do.

Sometimes the status helps, but it can work against me, too. I have to prove to everybody that I'm not just an ex-football player, that I know what I'm doing. If I do a bad job, it gets around a lot quicker. If John Doe messed up, nobody hears about it. Nobody cares. So I have to watch my back in the business.

I don't want someone to do business with me because of who I am, I want them to do business with me because of what I know. It goes back to college when I wanted to be paid for my brains, not my body. I don't want to be a hand-shaker. I don't want to be brought out to just finish off the deal. I always thought more highly of myself than that.

Heidi has some problems with my work at NIA. She was always a big part of my life, supporting me in my career. At NIA, it's hard for us to be a team.

"We have one product and that's Karl Nelson," she says. "We get along perfectly and we have a great marriage. He likes my ideas. At NIA, I can't help him at all. We go to charity events together, but we don't like to solicit business there. So I can't help him."

Heidi also thinks the job is boring, but it's a challenge to me every day. It's a straight commission job, so if you don't produce, you don't eat. That's a lot of pressure. Every month you start at zero. I'm lucky I have had the radio job.

I started doing the radio work in '87, during my radiation treatments, and it was all thanks to Jay Goldberg.

Heidi and I met Jay just before Super Bowl XXI at a Tomorrow's Children dinner honoring George Martin. We started talking and he said, "Boy, you have a great voice. Have you ever thought about broadcasting?"

I hadn't, but I like to keep my options open, so I said I'd think about it. But I was really thinking, Who is this little guy? What the hell does he know? I've got a deep voice and a lot of people like it, but I didn't see too much happening with it.

Still, we became friends. Heidi was working on a celebrity cookbook for Tomorrow's Children and Jay was helping her.

During my first two surgeries, Jay came to visit me every day. That's just the kind of warm, caring person he is. One day, he asked, "Would you like to do the Giants games on radio this year?"

I said, "If you can pull that off, it would be great."

The next thing I knew, he got me a contract with WNEW.

I missed the opening game in '87. It was in Chicago, and I wasn't ready to travel yet after the thoracotomy and laparotomy. I started my broadcast career the next week, a home game against the Dallas Cowboys.

I was more nervous two hours before air time than five minutes before. When the time came to put the headphones on, I wasn't nervous at all.

We lost that game—and it was "we," since I was still a player—and at the end of the broadcast I said, "I don't like this." I didn't mean to say it over the air, and people thought I was talking about broadcasting. I just meant I didn't like seeing the Giants lose, and especially not to Dallas.

I actually liked radio, even though it was a squeeze to get a word in. WNEW already had Jim Gordon doing the play-by-play and Dick Lynch, who played defensive back for some of the great Giants teams from 1959 to 1966, doing the analysis.

At first, I was only allowed to talk during extended time outs, during the two-minute warning and at half time, when I'd have a two-minute analysis piece. If I had something to say, I had to raise my hand and, if they had time, they'd get to me.

Still, I liked it. In '87, it kept me close to the team, close to the game. I was able to travel with the team and feel a little part of it. The radio work came naturally to me. As I talked more and more, I became better and better. Sometimes, I think announcers just talk to fill the dead air, but when I raised my hand, I had something important to add.

In '88, I went back to being a player, but when I was on IR with my bad ankle, I thought about asking to do the games again. Somehow, though, that wouldn't have seemed right. But WNEW told me that if I hung it up after the season, I had a job with them, so I was very encouraged. And when I knew I wasn't going to be playing in '89, I told Jay to contact them again.

I sneaked in again because I was sick, and I think they felt a little sorry for me. But I ended up being pretty good at it. Now, they can't get me out of there.

I've really enjoyed it, and I hope I have a future in broadcasting.

In '89, as the season went on, they let me talk more and more. I think Dick worked a little harder with me in the booth, too. It made him concentrate a little more on the game. The way we work it now, if it's a big play, I just shut up and let Dick talk. If it's just normal game action, I jump in, but I always glance over to make sure he's not going to start first. If I have something really important, I might hold up a finger and he'll let me talk. He's gotten very good about that.

Besides the game analysis, I started doing our pregame "Tailgate Show" during the '89 season. It's totally different, a fun thing. We're out in the parking lot, interviewing the fans before the game and running trivia contests and other games. I'll ride around on the back of a helmet-cart, like a king in his chariot, cruising the tailgate picnics with our own cheerleaders. You have to have an outgoing personality and be able to talk to people, and it's developing some different skills in me.

Bob Papa, my co-host, is really good, and Paul Dottino, our producer, does most of the work during the week setting things up. We just have a lot of fun.

On our first show, back in '89, they didn't have our broadcast platform ready until two minutes before air time. And that's how it's been, flying by the seat of our pants. Sometimes, interviewing those Giants fans can be tricky, but I'm proud that in four years of shows, we've never had one curse word go out on the air. The first year, we had more football analysis, interviewing out-of-town writers who would stop by our setup by the Meadowlands Racetrack, about 500 yards from Giants Stadium. But we found out that the lighter we keep it, the better the show is.

After 32 years, the Giants moved their broadcasts from WNEW to WOR Radio for the '93 season, and we expect to keep doing the "Tailgate Show." The fans love it. We get almost 1,000 people coming over to our broadcast location, and they really have to go out of their way to do it, since we're not allowed to set up closer to the stadium.

The sponsors love it, too. And Heidi loves it.

She's able to help me with the "Tailgate Show" the way she helped with football. During production meetings, she's come up with some great ideas for contests and games. And during the show, while Bob and I are doing our thing, she's in the parking lot with the sponsors. I don't have time for that, running right over to the stadium for the game broadcast as soon as we're done with the pregame, but she keeps them happy.

During the games, she has better seats now, right behind the Giants bench, and she gets to use the radio station's luxury box at Giants Stadium.

"When you're a player's wife," she says, "they treat you like you're not part of it, that you're not needed. When you're a broadcaster's wife, you're welcomed and you're respected. It's wonderful. I can have input and help make Karl's show better. People are very receptive to me."

People ask me if I miss football and I tell them I don't. Radio is great. You wake up the next morning and you're not sore. That's much easier on Heidi, not having to worry about me getting hurt.

Radio keeps me part of the team. I'm still associated with the Giants. And it got me to another Super Bowl.

The 1990 season, the first season I was no longer a professional football player, was fun. The Giants started out on a 10–0 roll and were fighting with the San Francisco 49ers for the NFC's spot in Super Bowl XXV.

Phil Simms, the best quarterback in the NFL that season, got hurt late in the year, but Jeff Hostetler came on for the final two games of the season and took the team to a 13–3 finish.

We beat the Chicago Bears in our first playoff game, then had to go out to San Francisco to play the 49ers at Candlestick Park for the NFC title.

We didn't score a touchdown. Leonard Marshall knocked Joe Montana out of the game with a brutal hit, and the defense forced a late turnover that set up Matt Bahr's fifth field goal for a 15-13 win.

There was no off-week between the conference championships and the Super Bowl that year, but I flew back home on a red-eye and then Heidi and I went to Tampa on the Giants' family charter Thursday before the game against the AFC champion Buffalo Bills.

For three days, we had a great time. We didn't worry about anything that had to do with football. We saw my grandparents and went to Busch Gardens. Bob Papa was doing updates for the station every hour and was locked in his room at the Hyatt, where we were all staying with the team. We'd just walk by and wave and head out for some fun.

On Sunday, we did the "Tailgate Show" from the NFC's hospitality tent by Tampa Stadium. There were a lot of eerie things going on. President Bush had just sent our troops into Desert Storm in the Middle East, and there was worry that there might be some kind of terrorist retaliation at the Super Bowl, America's biggest sporting event. There were helicopters patrolling the area, and anti-terrorist barricades set up to stop an attempted car-bomb from crashing in and exploding. On the roof at the stadium, you could see the sharpshooters with their rifles, ready just in case.

After the "Tailgate Show," we drove to the stadium in our rented Lincoln, with John Kennelly, another WNEW sports announcer, in the back. I think one of the security guards mistook "Kennelly" for "Kennedy," because when they waved us through, they said, "This way, Senator."

We went through the metal detectors they'd set up at the gates, then Heidi went to her seat and I headed up to the booth on top of the stadium.

I'll never forget the planes flying overhead, or the sea of little American flags waving in the stands, or Whitney Houston's rendition of the national anthem.

It was a great scene and a great game. The Giants held the ball for 40:33, a Super Bowl record. And Hostetler was tremendous.

Just a year before, we had spent Super Bowl Sunday in the Bahamas, watching San Francisco crush Denver. Merv Griffin's Resorts International had invited us down there and told me to bring a few friends. I asked Eric Dorsey, Bob Kratch, and Hostetler. We all gave our views of what was going to happen in the game, and then took questions from the audience. I don't remember anybody asking Jeff anything. In fact, we had problems when we said we wanted the Hostetlers with us. He was still just the backup quarterback and they didn't think he was a big enough name.

A year later, he was the Super Bowl hero.

Super Bowl XXV was really a great game to talk about, with lots of technical points to make. I remember one play especially,

Mark Ingram's catch and run on a third-and-13, twisting and turning and lunging for just enough to get the first down. That catch and run kept the Giants moving on a 75-yard, 14-play march towards a go-ahead touchdown that ate up the first 9:29 of the second half.

Just the other day, I was watching ESPN show the highlights of the past Super Bowls. And there was my voice-over on Ingram's catch. It synched up perfectly when they ran the play in slow motion.

I remember that play very clearly. And, of course, the ending when Buffalo's Scott Norwood missed a 37-yard field goal wide to the right, and the Giants won 20–19.

Jim Gordon set the scene and gave the call: "It's up and it's no good!"

And nobody said anything else.

I remember thinking, "Somebody's got to say something!"

So I started screaming, "Giants win! Giants win! Giants win!"

Everybody kidded me when we heard the replays of the call, but somebody had to say something. Jim is always very conscious of giving the crowd reaction, but I couldn't help myself.

That call and Ingram's catch are my two most vivid memories of the game. The Giants had won again, but the scene was a little different from Super Bowl XXI's rout.

After the game, I didn't have to worry about the crowds in the locker room. I stayed up in the broadcast booth, taking phone calls from Giants fans on our postgame "Point After" show. By the time we got done, the team had cleared out. So Heidi and I drove back to the hotel.

"Let's go to bed," I said.

"No way," she said. "We didn't celebrate the last time. We're going to do this one right."

So we went down to the hotel lobby. There was no official party and we were on our own, but we met Jerry Zaro, a lawyer we knew, and some of his friends, and we had a few cocktails with them.

Then we went upstairs to Parcells' party and crashed it.

There were a lot of rumors then about Bill leaving the team and Heidi walked right up and asked, "So, Bill, you coming back or what?"

He just laughed. Said, "Yeah, I think so."

He left four months later.

That party ended, but the night didn't. We stayed up straight through. The players were out doing their own thing and we didn't see many of them. We saw Hostetler the next morning when we were checking out, and he looked like he'd been worked over pretty good. I don't know if it was the beating he took during the game, or the partying he did after.

We had a good time. Super Bowl XXV was a lot more enjoyable for us than Super Bowl XXI.

It can take its toll, working five days a week at NIA and then the weekend on the radio. But it's a great part-time job. There are only 20 games counting the preseason, with half of them at home, and they treat you well.

I know one of the teams inside out, so I really only have to study the Giants' opponent. I do that for a few hours each week. I always considered myself a student of the game and my general football knowledge helps. I leave the fluff stuff to Dick. He dishes out the stats and the player's college backgrounds. When I talk, I talk football.

The radio job has kept me involved with the game and with the team. And I absolutely love it.

I don't know what the future holds. Heidi and I are working to get things back to normal for us and for Brittany and Lyndsay, our girls. We try to take a step at a time—forward, not backward.

After the radiation treatments, I had planned to play two or three more years. I always regretted not making the Pro Bowl. I had a season in '86 that I could have and maybe should have. But the Giants hadn't had an offensive lineman in the Pro Bowl since 1968, and they weren't going to take two tackles. Brad Benson, with that band-aid on his nose, had more notoriety, and he deserved it. He was a consistent player and one of the hardest working players I knew.

If I hadn't gotten cancer and missed '87, I would have made it, too. That was going to be my year, but I got sick and the Giants went 6–9. If I'd been on the team, I don't think they would have been that bad. Not just because of the way I played, but because of how losing me hurt our continuity on the offensive line.

Still, I know guys who have made the Pro Bowl and never won the Super Bowl and they all tell me, "Don't worry about that. You got the ring."

A Pro Bowl would have been nice, but when I retired I started thinking about what I'd accomplished. I'd played in 55 consecutive games, including the Super Bowl. I played some pretty good games against some pretty good players. Looking back, I was probably a better player than I thought I was.

On the field, I won the big one. Off the field, I won the biggest one.

It doesn't get much better than that.